SECRETS OF
MONET'S GARDEN

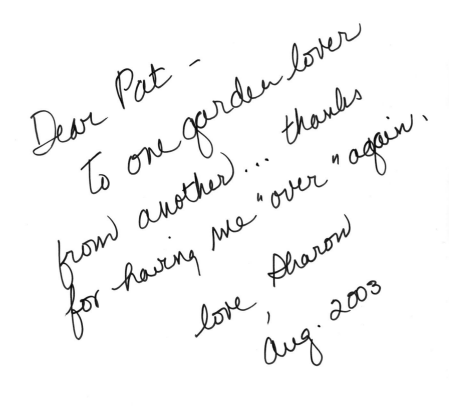

Dear Pat —
To one garden lover
from another ... thanks
for having me "over" again,
love, Sharon
Aug. 2003

SECRETS OF
MONET'S GARDEN

BRINGING THE BEAUTY OF MONET'S STYLE TO YOUR OWN GARDEN

Text and Photography

by Derek Fell

MetroBooks

MetroBooks

An Imprint of the
Michael Friedman Publishing Group, Inc.

2001 First MetroBooks Edition
©1997 by Michael Friedman Publishing Group, Inc.

Library of Congress Cataloging-in-Publication Data
available upon request.

ISBN 1-58663-193-4

Editor: Susan Lauzau
Art Director: Jeff Batzli
Design: Elan Studio
Photography Editors: Chris Bain and Amy Talluto

Color separations by Bright Arts Graphics (S) Pte Ltd.
Printed in Singapore by KHL Printing Co. Pte Ltd

10 9 8 7 6 5 4 3 2 1

For bulk purchases and special sales, please contact:
Michael Friedman Publishing Group, Inc.
Attention: Sales Department
230 Fifth Avenue
New York, NY 10001
212/685-6610 FAX 212/685-3916

Visit our website:
www.metrobooks.com

ACKNOWLEDGMENTS

MANY PEOPLE HELPED MAKE THIS BOOK POSSIBLE. MOST IMPORTANT IS MY WIFE, CAROLYN. A FORMER COLOR SPECIALIST FOR THE FASHION INDUSTRY WHO WORKED WITH PIERRE CARDIN AND CALVIN KLEIN, SHE REVIEWED MY RESEARCH INVOLVING MONET'S COLOR HARMONIES. THEODORE MONICA, PROFESSOR OF ART HISTORY, REVIEWED MY WORK ON MONET'S PAINTING TECHNIQUE AND ITS HISTORICAL CONTEXT. MICHAEL FRIEDMAN, MY PUBLISHER, REALIZED THE NEED FOR THE BOOK, AND BROUGHT A TEAM OF TALENTED EDITORS AND DESIGNERS TO THE PROJECT.

A BIG THANKS TO BARBARA DAVIES, OF STAPELEY WATER GARDENS IN ENGLAND, FOR MAKING A SPECIAL TRIP TO THE MARLIAC NURSERY IN FRANCE TO LOCATE INVOICES BETWEEN MARLIAC AND MONET (SHOWING PLANTS THAT MONET PURCHASED). I AM EQUALLY INDEBTED TO HIROSHI MAKITA, GARDEN DESIGNER, FOR EXPLAINING THE CONCEPT OF JAPANESE CUP GARDEN DESIGNS, AND TO JOHN BROWN, LANDSCAPE ARCHITECT, FOR FIRST LOANING ME THE ONLY KNOWN PAINTING OF MONET'S VEGETABLE GARDEN AND THEN AGREEING TO SELL IT TO ME.

THANKS ALSO TO KATHY NELSON, MY ASSISTANT, FOR ORGANIZING MY PHOTO FILES, AND WENDY FIELDS, MY GROUNDS SUPERVISOR, FOR TAKING CARE OF MY OWN GARDEN AT CEDARIDGE FARM WHILE I WAS AWAY RESEARCHING.

MONET HAD HIS MENTORS—EUGÈNE BOUDIN, THE SEASCAPE PAINTER, AND GUSTAVE CAILLEBOTTE, ARTIST, ART PATRON, AND MASTER GARDENER. MY OWN MENTORS ARE E. O'DOWD GALLAGHER, BRITISH FOREIGN CORRESPONDENT, WHO TAUGHT ME TO WRITE; THE LATE HARRY SMITH, BRITISH HORTICULTURAL PHOTOGRAPHER, WHO TAUGHT ME TO PHOTOGRAPH GARDENS; AND THE LATE DAVID BURPEE, DEAN OF AMERICAN SEEDSMEN, WHO TAUGHT ME A GREAT DEAL ABOUT PLANTS.

CONTENTS

FOREWORD ⮑ 8

INTRODUCTION ⮑ 10

Chapter One: BORROWING MONET'S GARDEN STYLE ⮑ 22

Chapter Two: MONET'S COLOR HARMONIES ⮑ 36

Chapter Three: MONET'S FAVORITE STRUCTURES ⮑ 50

Chapter Four: THE WATER GARDEN ⮑ 64

Chapter Five: THE CLOS NORMAND ⮑ 80

Chapter Six: THE VEGETABLE GARDEN ⮑ 94

Chapter Seven: TREES, SHRUBS, AND VINES ⮑ 102

Chapter Eight: MONET'S PLANT PALETTE ⮑ 116

CONCLUSION ⮑ 140

VISITING MONET'S GARDEN ⮑ 141

ABOUT THE AUTHOR ⮑ 142

SOURCES ⮑ 142

INDEX ⮑ 143

FOREWORD

"He has dared to create effects so true-to-life as to appear unreal, but which charm us irresistibly, as does all truth revealed. Who inspired all this? His flowers. Who was his teacher? His garden." —ARSENE ALEXANDRE, *LE FIGARO*, 1901

By Theodore R. Monica, Jr., Professor of Art History

Analyzing art history is often a process of osmosis. The opinions of one era, or of one expert, are contradicted by the opinions of another, until a final consensus of academic opinion becomes accepted. Therefore, the slightest new revelation is often cause for celebration in the art world.

Several books have attempted to analyze Monet's garden and his planting philosophy. In the rush to publish, a number of writers have made speculative or confusing comments and the subject is now rife with contradictions. Derek Fell's work, *Secrets of Monet's Garden*, is a breath of fresh air, sweeping aside some of the misinformation and presenting Monet's garden in its proper context—as a work of artistic merit, full of delightful color harmonies and other nuances that made his garden his greatest work of art.

Though Derek Fell is best known as a garden writer, he has an acute sense of artistry, from his work as North America's most widely published color photographer and from years of research for his works *Renoir's Garden* and *The Impressionist Garden*. For the first time, Monet's garden is presented with clear examples of the most important visual sensations that make the garden a magnificent work of art. Many historians believe that Monet's garden came from his art, but there is a weight of opinion that his art came from his appreciation of gardens. Monet himself declared that he owed his success as a painter to flowers.

In 1987, in an article called "The Zen of Gardening," for *Connoisseur* magazine, Derek wrote of Japanese landscape designer Hiroshi Makita: "He suffers like a painter or a sculptor over the tilt of a boulder or whether the moon will be reflected in the very center of a pool he is contemplating, for he too is an artist, whose materials are stones, trees, and water." Was this not also true of Monet, who declared an affiliation to Japanese artisans? The same article notes that gardens are less marketable than fine paintings and sculpture. "Leave a picture in the attic and it can increase in value with no effort on the part of the owner, but neglect a garden for only a few weeks and it starts to revert to wilderness," Fell writes. It is this ephemeral quality that often causes us to overlook the artistry of gardens.

The miracle of Monet's garden is not only that the garden survived more than half a century of neglect before its remarkable restoration, but that such clear insights into the working of the garden as an artistic masterpiece are now being presented.

Thank you, Derek Fell, for this thoroughly enjoyable, enlightening insight into Monet's garden, packed with so many useful ideas to making our own garden spaces more enjoyable.

INTRODUCTION

"Nothing is more the child of art than a garden."
—SIR WALTER SCOTT

Monet's garden, in Giverny, France, is the most visited garden of its size in the western world. Located just north of Paris, the 5-acre (2-hectare) property attracts nearly half a million visitors annually. The allure of Monet's garden is not only the extraordinary beauty packed into such a small area, but also the enigma of Monet himself, the historical significance of his garden in the world of art, and the universal popularity of his glorious Impressionist paintings.

Throughout his painting career and a life that spanned eighty-six years, from 1840 to 1926, Monet was strangely insecure about his work. Perhaps the ridicule heaped upon his early paintings and the years of financial struggle with a large family to support made him insular and uncomfortable discussing the source of his hard-won success. He was secretive about his work, and he was even more secretive about his garden, which he considered his greatest work of art. Sensing a pending discussion about art appreciation in a meeting with one of his most important patrons, the Duc de Trévise, Monet warned, "Don't ask me for advice. I give none of it to anyone." In fact, he was the antithesis of fellow painter Vincent van Gogh, who wrote reams of letters about many of his paintings and what inspired them, even explaining precisely what he admired about a particular garden or landscape he painted.

BRUSH STROKES OF COLOR

Except for a brief explanation of the reflective quality of his pond and the role his water lilies played in his overall scheme, Monet wrote and discussed little about his gardening philosophy. He planted his garden to paint, using plants like brush strokes; he pronounced himself good for only two things

Above: *Monet's bedroom window offers an overall view of the Clos Normand and its arched footpath, the Grande Allée. This part of the garden features lots of color, especially in autumn when many annuals and perennials reach maturity.* **Opposite:** *Monet loved to visit Le Jardin des Plantes, in Rouen, where he evaluated new varieties of plants. Monet sought the advice of its director before installing a greenhouse on his property.*

in life—painting and gardening. In a letter to the local township supervisors, requesting permission to expand his water garden, he declared that its purpose was for painting, among other objectives. The letter reads, "It is only a question of something for amusement, and for the pleasure of the eyes, and also with a view to motifs for painting." Though he knew he wanted to create planting schemes to paint, at this early planning stage he seems to have had few specifics in mind. A later letter states, "It took me some time to understand my water lilies. I had planted them for pleasure, I cultivated them without thinking of painting them." He seems to have worked doggedly at his garden, experimenting with color schemes, retaining and embellishing those ideas that pleased him. As the garden was brought to perfection, its fame as a unique landscape and a magnificent work of art spread throughout the art world, but it was left to others to unravel or relate its mysteries and secrets.

PAINTERS IN THE GARDEN

Fortunately, Monet did allow some astute observers to see his fantastic garden, and since he was so protective of his privacy, it was considered a great honor to be allowed through the entrance gate and beyond the garden's stout stone wall

Every Monday Monet's garden at Giverny is closed to the public in order to allow artists freedom to paint and gardeners the time to do maintenance work. Before beginning to paint, artists must request a permit.

enclosure. Though Monet discouraged painters from visiting his garden, he welcomed art patrons, journalists, art critics, and close friends such as fellow Impressionist painters Pierre-Auguste Renoir, Paul Cézanne, and Gustave Caillebotte.

Most of what we know about Monet's gardening philosophy comes from correspondence and published magazine articles. Especially enlightening are accounts by his children (particularly his stepson, Jean-Michel Hoschedé, who wrote a book about Monet) and the French garden writer Georges Truffaut. A botanist, soil scientist, and nurseryman, Truffaut advised Monet not only on where to locate plants and how to grow them, but also on improving pockets of alkaline soil by adding massive amounts of manure and peat moss. One observer noted, "The garden lay on a gentle slope facing the valley of the Seine to the south. It was warm and sunny, but the chalk subsoil was near the surface and the beds needed much attention."

The Grande Allée in late summer shows rampant nasturtiums almost meeting in the middle of the walk. Monet first used nasturtiums this way in his garden at Vétheuil.

Some of Truffaut's firsthand accounts of Monet's garden are remarkably detailed. Writing in 1924 for the French magazine *Jardinage*, in an article entitled "The Gardens of a Great Painter," Truffaut begins by telling us: "In 1883, the eminent painter Claude Monet created a series of gardens in Giverny, near Vernon, which have become justifiably famous and have enabled him to compose the best-known pictures now unfortu-nately scattered in America and Germany.... The Giverny gardens are made up of three groups: the Clos Normand, the water garden, and the vegetable garden." Truffaut then describes the highlights of each season, starting with the mass flowering of daffodils and cherry trees in the spring.

The restoration of Monet's garden through the remarkable energies of Gerald van der Kemp and his wife, Florence, has helped shed more light on Monet's planting philosophy. But in some ways it has also helped to obscure it, as an army of contemporary authors and photographers has since descended upon the property. Presented with such an extravagance of riches, writers have not always put the right interpretation on a planting scheme. In the text that follows, therefore, I try to make a clear distinction between conjecture and fact, faithful replication and true experimentation.

Many books have been written about Monet's life at Giverny, his paintings, and his garden. The best information tends to come from the work of Claire Joyes, wife of Jean-Marie Toulgouat, Madame Monet's great-grandson (he is descended from the marriage of Monet's stepdaughter to the American Impressionist painter Theodore Butler). The Toulgouats live a short distance from Monet's house, and in the spring of 1989 I had the pleasure of spending a day with them.

MONET'S SOURCES

Locating Monet's sources for plants and identifying specific varieties sometimes requires detective work. For example, in a letter to his friend Georges Clemenceau (former premier of France) in 1923, Monet states that he is planning to send him some Pennsylvania roses. Monet's main sources for plants were nurseries in France, Holland, England, and Japan, but here is an indication that he also counted at least one American nursery—Conard and Jones—among his sources.

Nor are art historians always correct in their analysis of Monet's garden portrayals. For example, his painting *Bend in the River Epte* (1888) is sometimes considered an example of Pointillism, a style in which dots of color create an overall scene, rather like the dot screen printing process used in modern color printing. In fact, Monet disliked Pointillism and said so, stating quite bluntly "there are no points in nature." At a glance the painting does look vaguely Pointillist, but actually it is a wonderful traditional Impressionist rendering of the wind blowing through poplar leaves, making them shimmer. The painting offers a classic example of the way the great Impressionist painters loved to capture a special moment of light.

I first became curious about Monet's garden in 1980 when I learned that Mrs. Lila Acheson Wallace, publisher of *Reader's Digest* magazine, had donated $1 million to restore the garden. I realized it would take time for the new plantings to mature, so I didn't visit until the spring of 1989. Following a trip in early

Above: *The climbing rose 'American Pillar' scrambles vigorously up one of the arches beside Monet's water garden. Undoubtedly, Monet obtained this popular cultivar from Pennsylvania rose growers Conard and Jones (now the Conard-Pyle Company). Monet liked the rose so much that he offered cuttings of it to his friend Clemenceau, former premier of France.* **Opposite:** *In early May, Monet's water garden features islands of water lily foliage just starting to form on the surface of the pond.*

May to some Dutch bulb fields and then the van Gogh Museum in Amsterdam, I took the train to Paris and saw the garden at a peak flowering time, when all the wallflowers, tulips, primroses, pansies, and Dutch irises were in full bloom.

Following that first visit, several lucky events gave me further insights into Monet's garden. In 1990, I visited the south of France to photograph Renoir's garden, near Nice. Monet and Renoir were life-long friends, and though their garden philosophies differ, the study of one helps explain the other. Similarly, a study I made of Cézanne's restored garden at Aix-en-Provence helped me understand nuances of Monet's garden that are easily overlooked. Both Monet and Renoir were friends of Cézanne, and they visited him in Provence.

For years I was told that the French nursery Latour-Marliac, which hybridized Monet's water lilies, was no longer in business. But Patrick Nutt, the retired water lily specialist at Longwood Gardens, introduced me to the new owners, Bill and Barbara Davies. The Davies encouraged me to stay overnight in the historic nursery and located for me invoices from the nursery to Monet that date back to 1894.

Above: *Joseph Latour-Marliac (inset) hybridized his famous water lilies at his nursery at Temple-sur-Lot, near Bordeaux.* **Opposite:** *Founded in 1875, the Latour-Marliac Nursery looks today exactly as it did a hundred years ago when Monet began collecting Marliac's water lily hybrids. The shallow pots stand ready to be filled with soil and water lily roots; they are then submerged beneath the water.*

PERFECT PARTNERS

OLD-FASHIONED 'BARNHAVEN' PRIMROSES — PARTNERED WITH THE NODDING, CUP-SHAPED BLOOMS OF LENTEN ROSES (*Helleborus orientalis*) — GROW BESIDE MONET'S POND IN EARLY SPRING. GERTRUDE JEKYLL FIRST STARTED HYBRIDIZING PRIMROSES AT HER HOME, MUNSTEAD WOOD, IN ENGLAND. FROM THIS PIONEER WORK, MS. FLORENCE BELLIS DEVELOPED THE IMPROVED 'BARNHAVEN' STRAIN, WORKING FROM HER HOME NEAR PORTLAND, OREGON. HER STRAINS OF PRIMROSES WERE TRANSFERRED TO A BRITISH NURSERY ON HER RETIREMENT, AND THEN TO A FRENCH NURSERY IN BRITTANY, WHERE THE PUREST STRAINS OF 'BARNHAVEN' PRIMROSES ARE NOW PRODUCED.

THE PINK HOUSE

Many people are aware of Monet's two ornamental gardens—the Clos Normand, an English-style flower garden, and the water garden, Monet's interpretation of a Japanese garden—which are extensions of his home, affectionately called the Pink House for the color of its walls. The walls are in fact a beige stucco infused with brick dust to create a pink hue. This house occupies a commanding position at the top of the gently sloping garden, and creates an ideal background for flowering plants. The overall effect is of a pink haze, reminiscent of hazes that Monet noted on trips to the South of France.

THE BLUE HOUSE

Few people are aware that Monet also cultivated an ambitious 2½-acre (1-hectare) vegetable garden on a separate property, located at the other end of Giverny village. Monet called this property on the Rue de Chein the Blue House, and referred to the garden as his "formal garden," since it featured both flowers and edible plants in large geometric beds. There is a brief description of this potager in *Monet's Table* by Claire Joyes, but no painting or photograph showed what it looked like. On a visit to Giverny I located the site, which has been divided up into several properties, and found the gardener's house still intact, complete with blue stucco walls and stout stone enclosures, which Monet covered with espaliered fruit trees. Interestingly, the front yard of the Blue House is planted predominantly with pink roses and pink-flowering perennials, creating one of Monet's favorite color combinations—blue and pink.

Following publication of my book *The Impressionist Garden,* in which I showed a photograph of the site, I received a visit from landscape designer John Brown, who had acquired at a Sotheby's auction the only known painting of Monet's vegetable garden. Painted by American Impressionist painter Willard Metcalf, it shows the garden in spring with beds of lettuce and cabbage laid out in a quiltlike pattern, each bed completely surrounded by double rows of peonies in full bloom.

INFLUENCES ON MONET'S GARDENING STYLE

Monet was greatly influenced in his appreciation of gardens by Gustave Caillebotte, a wealthy art patron as well as a painter with a passion for strong lines of perspective.

The design of Caillebotte's own garden, with its retangular planting beds, regimented lines of espaliered fruit trees, and standard-form roses, helped Monet realize that his garden at Giverny should also have strong lines of perspective, even though he planted it in the exuberant style of an English cottage garden. The extent of Caillebotte's influence can be judged not only from

Above: *A bush of old-fashioned single pink roses is set off beautifully by the vibrant stucco face of the Blue House.* **Opposite:** *The Pink House's dusky rose facade is the perfect backdrop for a pink and red motif using tulips and English daisies.*

studying these painters' affectionate correspondence, but also by visiting the site of Caillebotte's earliest garden paintings—his family's estate at Yerres, near what is now Orly airport.

Though the vegetable garden had reportedly been destroyed to make room for a municipal parking lot, I wanted to see for myself. Indeed, I found the garden only partially gone. A good portion still is cultivated as a bountiful vegetable garden, including the section portrayed in Caillebotte's early masterpiece, *The Gardeners* (1876).

Horticulturists and art historians have long wondered whether the British garden designer Gertrude Jekyll had any influence on Monet, or vice versa, even speculating that they may have met. A eulogy to Miss Jekyll, written by Professor Christopher Tunnard for an architectural publication shortly after Miss Jekyll's death, compared her life to that of Monet: "Both had an almost primitive love of the soil, a passion for gathering from Nature the nourishment to sustain burning convictions and long cherished beliefs.... Both suffered from failing

Pronounced lines of perspective, all leading toward the house, characterize the Clos Normand. The long, parallel flower beds are edged with low-growing, lavender-blue aubretia and filled with lilies, poppies, irises, and other flowers. Strategically placed small trees, including crab apples and cherries, punctuate the expansive beds.

eyesight and both achieved greatness through work and love of tools and methods they employed." The "fundamental difference between them," he declared, was that "Monet's garden was as great as his paintings, while Jekyll's paintings were inferior to her plantings, particularly in her treatment of light and Monet's success at infusing his garden with the impressionist shimmer." However, Tunnard accorded her the honor of calling her the first horticultural Impressionist.

Actually, there are other distinct differences in the planting styles of Jekyll and Monet. In many ways, Monet's finesse as a colorist goes well beyond Jekyll's color theories. Monet's innovative use of vines strung along metal frames to create the sensation of a lace-curtain effect, his fascination with the translucent qualities of flowers, and his liking for blue and mauve flowers to improve shady areas all show him to be an inspired and imaginative gardener.

In late summer, annuals, perennials, and vines bloom in profusion in Monet's cottage-style flower garden.

This book strives not only to correct some of the contradictions and inconsistencies in previous books about Monet's garden, but to delve deeper into his design philosophy. In the creation of his Clos Normand flower garden Monet was greatly influenced by the English rebellion against formality in planting schemes, such as carpet bedding. "But for the countryside, he prefers an English garden to a forest," declared writer Emile Zola. For his extraordinary water garden, however, Monet created his own interpretation of a classic Japanese cup garden design. Also presented here is a detailed review of Monet's favorite color harmonies, such as the coupling of yellow and blue ("the gold and sapphire of an artist's dreams," identified by art critic Wynford Dewhurst), and even some sensational triadic color combinations, such as red-silver-green and blue-pink-white.

In studying Monet's garden it helps to look at it not only in a historical context—as the garden of a great Impressionist painter—but also in a horticultural context. Monet brought to gardening a knowledge of plants, a particular passion for flow-

ers, and a painter's appreciation of color and form. Marcel Proust, writing in *Le Figaro*, France's leading newspaper, perhaps said it best when he declared that Monet's garden was "less a flower garden than a color garden." In other words, the flowers are the means to an end. Artists the world over have found that a study of Monet's use of flowers provides a better understanding of his art. The two are inseparable. His stepdaughter, Blanche, reported to the Duc de Trévise that not a day went by that Monet did not take three or four turns along his garden paths. To Trévise himself, Monet declared, "More than anything I must have flowers, always, always...."

The thrill of unlocking the secrets of Monet's garden has improved my work as both a photographer and a painter, and, most importantly, it has provided inspiration for planting themes in my own garden. The results of that inspiration are viewed each year by the thousands of visitors who come to visit Cedaridge Farm, and I've included details and scenes in this book that show how you can interpret Monet's vision in your own garden.

Chapter One

BORROWING MONET'S GARDEN STYLE

"I've grown used to the flowers in my

garden in the spring and to the water lilies in

my pond on the Epte in the summertime.

They give flavor to my life every day."

—CLAUDE MONET

Monet's Clos Normand flower garden in late spring features a profusion of peonies and bearded irises growing along parallel beds called *plante bands*.

CLEMENT GREENBERG, AN ART CRITIC, ONCE DESCRIBED AN IMPRESSIONIST PAINTING AS "A FOAMING, POURING, SHIMMERING PROFUSION LIKE NOTHING ELSE IN PAINTING; PICTURES THAT ARE SPOTTED AND WOVEN WITH SOFT POROUS COLORS, AND LOOK IN THEMSELVES LIKE SOFT BOUQUETS OF FLOWERS." THOUGH HE WAS DESCRIBING THE EFFECTS OF PAINT, IT IS AN APT DESCRIPTION OF MONET'S GARDEN. IF YOU WANT TO HAVE A GARDEN EXACTLY LIKE MONET'S, THE SHORT ANSWER IS THAT YOU PROBABLY CAN'T. AT LEAST NOT IN THE WAY THE GARDEN IS NOW PLANTED AND MANAGED, AS A COMPLEX SPACE WITH INTENSE COLOR THROUGH THREE SEASONS AND EVERY INCH OF SOIL VIBRANT WITH HEALTHY PLANTS. UNLESS YOU ARE PREPARED TO EMPLOY NINE GARDENERS WHO WORK LIKE DERVISHES UNDER THE EAGLE EYE OF A HEAD GARDENER, IT'S UNLIKELY YOU WILL BE ABLE TO REPLICATE THE FULL GRANDEUR OF GIVERNY. ALSO, YOU WOULD NEED TO USE A BACKHOE TO COMPLETELY DIG UP EXHAUSTED PLANTING BEDS FOR RENOVATION AND REPLANTING ALMOST EVERY YEAR. YOU'D ALSO REQUIRE A RANGE OF GREENHOUSES TO GROW NEARLY TWO HUNDRED THOUSAND ANNUALS, BIENNIALS, AND PERENNIALS. INSTEAD, IT IS MORE REALISTIC TO ADAPT MONET'S STYLISTIC CHOICES AND PLANTING PHILOSOPHIES FOR YOUR OWN BACKYARD. WHILE THE SCALE OF MONET'S GARDEN IS RATHER DAUNTING, HIS FAVORITE THEMES, ACCENTS, AND PLANTS CAN ALL BE EASILY BORROWED TO CREATE A LUSH, IMAGINITIVE GARDEN. THROUGHOUT THIS BOOK YOU'LL FIND DOZENS OF IDEAS FOR INCORPORATING THE BEAUTY OF MONET'S PLANTINGS INTO GARDENS THAT YOU CAN EASILY MAINTAIN.

GAINING INSPIRATION FROM GIVERNY

Today, Monet's greatest masterpiece—the world's most ephemeral work of art—lives on and brings pleasure to millions. Even with the hoards of tourists who visit daily, traffic through the garden is carefully regulated so you can study the work of the master and learn to emulate his revolutionary ideas on a smaller scale. You do not need six 40-foot (12-meter) metal spans to create a flowering tunnel such as his Grande Allée. You can achieve a similar effect with just one or two small spans.

Even the magical water garden can be reduced to the size of a whiskey barrel if all the space you have is a deck or patio. And many of Monet's spectacular color schemes look sensational arranged in pots. Try the red-pink-silver motif for a start.

Throughout the pages of this book, under the heading "Perfect Partners," are examples that show how the main ideas from Monet's garden can be used at home, with just two or three combinations of plants.

Today, Monet would probably be delighted that seventy years after his death his garden not only survives, it positively

A MONET-STYLE GARDEN

This small-space garden is based on Monet's Giverny design, and preserves the garden's primary elements but scales them for a typical backyard. Mix and match the features to suit your location. Here, a rose arch leads from the house to a tranquil water garden enclosed by screens of fast-growing river birch and hardy bamboo. Arches like these can be purchased from local garden centers or through mail-order catalogs. The 'Heritage' strain of river birch grows at the rate of 5 to 6 feet (1.5 to 1.8 meters) a year, so you'll soon have a beautiful grove, and the tree has the added benefits of decorative bark and shimmering leaves. The water garden is easily installed using a flexible liner to hold the water. If you have the room, include a small bridge and a bench from which to view your garden.

PLANT LIST

1. **Climbing rose** (*Rosa* 'American Pillar')
2. **Yellow groove bamboo** (*Phyllostachys aureosulcata*)
3. **Ostrich fern** (*Mattheucia strutheropteris*)
4. **Primrose** (*Primula × polyanthus*)
5. **Hardy water lily** (*Nymphaea × marliaca*)
6. **Hosta** (*Hosta sieboldiana* 'Elegans')
7. **Lady's mantle** (*Alchemilla mollis*)
8. **Peony** (*Paeonia lactiflora*)
9. **Meadowfoam** (*Limnanthes douglasii*)
10. **Lupine** (*Lupinus* 'Russell')
11. **Flag iris** (*Iris pseudacorus*)
12. **Japanese coltsfoot** (*Petasites japonicas* 'Gigantea')
13. **Astilbe** (*Astilbe × arendsi*)
14. **Weeping Japanese cut-leaf maple** (*Acer japonica* 'Dissectum')
15. **Japanese iris** (*Iris ensata*)
16. **Forget-me-not** (*Myosotis sylvatica*)
17. **Azalea** (*Rhododendron* 'Exbury')
18. **Rhododendron** (*Rhododendron* 'Ironclad')
19. **Heritage river birch** (*Betula nigra* 'Heritage')
20. **Golden chain tree** (*Laburnum × vossii*)

thrives, and that the secrets it contains are being unraveled. The puzzle he seemed reluctant to explain while he lived is now being solved, and the secrets of his methods and inspiration can be more fully understood by new generations of gardeners seeking to take their smaller Edens to new heights of visual excitement.

The following pages present Monet's planting philosophy in the form of usable ideas. Sometimes more than one idea can be combined to create a special effect. For example, the sensation of glitter can be achieved by planting white flowers liberally throughout the garden. To this can be added fleecy foliage, translucent blooms, bicolored flowers, and iridescent plants. Combine all five of these elements into a planting plan and the total effect is a remarkable glittering, shimmering, sparkling, glimmering appearance—an effect that is almost dazzling, and which seems to have caught the eye of Monet's visitors even more than his treasury of color harmonies. Typical is a comment by Monet's friend Octave Mirbeau, who wrote, "...the dahlias are stars that tremble and twinkle atop fragile branching stems ...the air is filled with so much glimmering, so much quivering."

THE SENSATION OF SHIMMER

No painter before or since Monet has captured the nuances of water so exquisitely. Indeed, he built a special studio boat so he could paint the Seine and its tributaries from alluring midstream vantage points. Whether painting a choppy seascape from the Normandy cliffs or a tranquil duck pond on a village green, Monet was the master of water. One of his favorite anecdotes centered on the English landscape painter J.M.W. Turner, who lashed himself to a ship's mast to paint a storm at sea.

An effect Monet loved to paint over and over was the shimmer of wavelets catching the sun's brightness and creating the sensation of glitter, from a thousand pinpricks of light dancing on the water. Like his paintings of glittering water, the sensation of shimmer set Monet's garden apart more than any

Opposite: *This cool-color harmony, which uses mauve 'Blue Parrot' tulips and blue forget-me-nots, is enlivened with shimmering white* Cerastium tomentosum *sprinkled liberally at ground level, and also with white* Clematis montana *blossoms cascading from a metal frame.*

PERFECT PARTNERS

THE BICOLORED, SINGLE-FLOWERED TULIP 'IBIS' BLAZES AMONG YELLOW SIBERIAN WALLFLOWERS, BLUE MOUNTAIN CORNFLOWERS, AND ORANGE PANSIES IN A SENSATIONAL COLOR COMBINATION. BOLD WHITE STREAKS ON THE TULIP SERVE TO ACCENTUATE ALL THE OTHER COLORS. VIGOROUS GREEN FOLIAGE ALSO INTENSIFIES THIS HOT COLOR PLANTING.

other planting technique. His layout in the Clos Normand flower garden not only produced the pronounced lines of perspective he wanted, but the regimented rectangular beds created the effect of waves of color, like surf rolling in from the ocean. All that was needed to imitate the frothiness of rolling surf or the sparkle of a wind-whipped lake was the liberal use of white. Not white planted in big bold clumps, but sprinkled lightly throughout the garden, using plants with airy flowers like dame's rocket, baby's breath, and feverfew.

Monet knew from his painting technique (which uses small, thick brush strokes of color to build up the canvas) that spots of white not only produce a shimmering effect, but also brighten bolder colors. For example, blue and red can look dull when used alone in a garden, but when placed next to white the primaries are enlivened. This effect can also be seen in flowers that have white centers or edges—the white center of a blue delphinium enhances the blue, making a mass of bicolored delphiniums look brighter than a solid sheet of blue. White can also serve as a link between colors that normally don't combine well together, such as purple and blue.

BICOLORED FLOWERS

The pleasing result of flecks of white brightening an adjacent color on canvas helped Monet realize that the same principle applied to bicolored flowers in his garden. Tulips and bearded irises are good examples of flowers that have been much hybridized, not only producing the most extensive range of colors in all the plant kingdom (with the exception of orchids), but also generating some wonderful bicolored flowers. When one of the two colors is white, its reflective quality adds to the sensation of shimmer. But bicolored flowers produce wonderful glimmer even when neither of the colors is white—red and yellow, pink and mauve, and other combinations also furnish a glittering sensation.

Monet's painting of iris beds, *Monet's Garden at Giverny* (1890), captures the glimmering effect produced by bicolored flowers. Though a casual glance seems to show a solid mass of purples and blues, a closer inspection of the painting reveals that the borders are composed of several iris hybrids featuring white upper petals and lower petals in a solid color.

PERFECT PARTNERS

MANY OF MONET'S BEARDED IRISES WERE BICOLORS—HE ESPECIALLY LOVED THE COMBINATION OF BLUE AND WHITE. THE CONTRAST OF WHITE MAKES THE BLUE PETALS SEEM TO SPARKLE, ADDING TO THE SHIMMERING SENSATION IN THE GARDEN. HERE, SIDE BY SIDE IN A BLUE AND ORANGE COLOR HARMONY, ARE TWO EXAMPLES OF BICOLORED BEARDED IRISES. THE IRIS ON THE LEFT, 'MARGARITE', FEATURES WHITE MARKINGS CONCENTRATED IN THE TOP OUTWARD-FACING PETALS, WHILE THE CULTIVAR IN THE MIDDLE, 'STEPPING OUT', HAS PATCHES OF WHITE ON BOTH THE UPPER AND LOWER PETALS. THE IRIS ON THE RIGHT IS A DUTCH IRIS IN A NEARLY SOLID BLUE; NOTE THE WAY IT ALMOST DISAPPEARS NEXT TO THE SPARKLING BICOLORS!

LACE CURTAIN EFFECTS

Monet had a passion for lace. He wore shirts with lace fronts and cuffs, and every window of his house was hung with lace curtains. He also introduced into his garden a lace curtain effect by training vines with white flowers (such as *Clematis montana* and *Polygonum aubertii*) high on metal frames. This not only added to the shimmering quality of his garden, but extended color above the garden so that when painting he would find his entire view vibrant with color. The lace curtain effect reaches its most spectacular heights in the water garden, where wisterias are threaded over a metal canopy covering Monet's Japanese bridge. The canopy blooms first with lavender-blue wisteria, then with later-flowering white wisteria.

For a brief period in early May, both the white and mauve wisteria are in flower along the canopy of Monet's Japanese-style bridge. The purple wisteria will fade first, leaving the later-blooming white variety to carry the show alone.

BRILLIANCE AND PURITY

When you look at an Impressionist painting, particularly a Monet, you realize that one of the elements that sets it apart from anything else in the art world is its brilliance and purity of color. Monet was struck by the fact that in nature certain flowers have colors so pure and brilliant they are almost impossible to render with paint. This is true of many of his favorite flowers, particularly red poppies, yellow tulips, and orange African daisies. The petals of these singular flowers are not only extraordinarily bright, they shine like satin. Monet loved them because they reflected light so intensely, and a liberal planting of these flowers throughout his garden added immeasurably to its brilliance, clarity, and purity.

BACKLIGHTING

Another quality that enabled Monet to present a glittering effect was backlighting. Certain flowers—such as cosmos and poppies—have transparent petals, and when backlit by the sun, the blooms take on a beautiful translucent quality that recalls the glow of Chinese lanterns. The effect is lessened

Above: *Oriental poppies* (Papaver orientale) *have petals that shine with a high gloss. This cultivar, 'Turkin Louise', has frilly petals in a vivid red-orange.* **Right:** *Single-flowered opium poppies* (P. somniferum) *glow when backlit by the sun. This translucent quality is lost in double varieties because the layered petals create an opaque effect. Here, the pale poppies produce a silvery gleam, while reds and pinks from phlox, hollyhocks, and roses combine in a stunning color harmony. Monet's second studio, now an administration office, is visible in the background.*

when flowers are double, not only because extra layers of petals diminish the translucence, but because double flowers are generally heavier. Instead of holding their heads up to the rays of the sun, the flowers become top-heavy and hang down, further reducing the translucent effect.

BLACK AND WHITE IN THE GARDEN

Curiously, a recent book about Monet's garden states that Monet hated black. Nothing could be further from the truth, and in fact, Monet's masterpiece *The Magpie* (1868–1869) has as its subject a black and white bird in a snow-covered garden. The huge canvas startled the art community with its monumental black and white motif, and it was promptly purchased by Caillebotte for his private collection. Today, the painting occupies a place of honor in the Orsay Museum in Paris. Caillebotte was the first Impressionist to plant a black and white color harmony, clearly seen in his painting *Artist's Studio Overlooking the Garden, Spring* (1882), which depicts a circular bed of black, maroon, cream, and white pansies under what appears to be a pink-flowering chestnut tree.

The exhibition of **The Magpie (1868–1869),** *Monet's most famous black and white color harmony, stimulated a frenzy of winter painting among other Impressionists. Monet extended this color theme to the garden as well, where he planted black or deep maroon flowers.*

In the garden, Monet realized that black can enhance bright colors, especially yellow, orange, and white, making these difficult-to-use colors more appealing. Black is an excellent complement to white, and when white or pale-colored flowers are clustered together there is no better way to temper the glare than to plant black flowers with them. Although many "black" flowers appear to be a deep maroon when observed in bright light, from a distance they look black, especially on cloudy days. To honor Monet's sensational magpie painting and his use of black flowers, the gardeners at Giverny today plant many black and white motifs. When black interrupts the glare of white, the sensation of shimmer is only increased.

In nature, there are actually some flowers that are both black and white, so you don't always have to seek solid black flowers to contrast with whites. Some particularly good black and white flowers to consider are 'Perry's White' Oriental poppies (*Papaver orientale* 'Perry's White'), 'Zulu' cape daisies (*Venidium fastuosum* 'Zulu'), 'White with Black Blotch' garden pansies (*Viola × wittrockiana* 'White with Black Blotch'), and *Nemophila* 'Penny Black'.

BLUE FOR SHADE

Monet realized that in nature shadows are rarely black, since a true black is produced by the total lack of light. Monet preferred instead to represent darkness with a mixture of colors. For example, he would paint in colors complementary to the colors casting the shadows. One of his favorite colors for shadows was blue, as in his painting *Field of Yellow Irises* (1887), in which he portrays a meadow of yellow flag irises, using blue shadows to complement the petal colors.

Monet took this idea of blue shadows into his garden by planting shady areas with blue flowers; he was particularly fond of blue forget-me-nots, bearded irises, agapanthus, and Spanish bluebells. Blue-flowering plants look sensational encircling a deciduous tree that allows dappled light to filter down; they also work well planted in great drifts along shaded paths.

Other colors that combine well with blue in shady areas are pink and mauve. Today at Giverny the gardeners use pink and mauve English daisies in combination with blue forget-me-nots; they also plant mixtures of pansies in shades of blue and mauve.

SINGLE AND DOUBLE FLOWERS

Contrary to several published reports, Monet's liking for single flowers (those flowers with a single row of petals) had nothing whatsoever to do with the hybridized look of many doubles (those with more than a single row of petals), since he cherished hybrids. A more plausible explanation for his special fondness for single flowers is the fact that they have better translucence than doubles when backlit and they have better reflective qualities when frontlit.

Perky, single cosmos flowers have sheer petals that seem to twinkle when backlit, while the adjacent double-flowered red dahlias are opaque, and hang their heavy heads.

PERFECT PARTNERS

BLUE FORGET-ME-NOTS AND MAUVE PANSIES GROW IN THE SHADE BENEATH AN ARBOR OF WISTERIA. THIS PAIRING EXEMPLIFIES MONET'S FONDNESS FOR PLANT-ING SHADY SPOTS WITH BLUE FLOWERS, TO BRING OUT THE BLUE TONES HE SAW IN SHADOWS.

Although Monet expressed a dislike for variegated foliage, it can be beautiful when used simply. In fact, the gardeners at Giverny today plant variegated bishop's weed to create a silvery edging for yellow 'West Point' lily-flowered tulips.

STRONG GREENS AND VARIEGATED FOLIAGE

We know from *Claude Monet*, the biography by Monet's stepson, Jean-Pierre Hoschedé, that Monet disliked variegated foliage, but we don't know why. Perhaps it was because he thought it looked anemic. Monet preferred leafy plants with strong, vigorous, healthy-looking leaf colors—rich dark greens and lustrous bronzes, for example. Archival photographs show that he grew 'Bishop of Llandaff' dahlias and 'Empress of India' nasturtiums, both of which have bold, bronze foliage.

HYBRID FLOWERS

Monet's dislike of double flowers and variegated foliage obviously had nothing to do with any "hybridized" quality, as some writers have claimed, because Monet collected hybrids for his garden, and his garden would have been lost without them. He visited flower shows, botanical gardens (especially the Jardin des Plantes, in Rouen), and the test gardens of specialist seedsmen and nurseries (even paying personal visits to Thompson & Morgan and Kelways

Nurseries in England), seeking out their finest hybrids, notebook in hand. Mrs. Violet Boone, a long-retired employee of Thompson & Morgan, remembers Monet being conducted ceremoniously around the company's trial gardens, stopping at every plot and making careful notes about anything that caught his fancy.

All Monet's water lilies were hybrids, which he procured from the leading French water lily hybridizer, Joseph Bory Latour-Marliac. Monet's two sons even hybridized a large red poppy they named 'Monet', but which has since been lost to cultivation.

WILDFLOWERS—THE SOUL OF THE GARDEN

Wildflowers were dear to Monet and he painted them whenever he found large colonies growing in meadows and swamps beyond his garden, introducing many to his flower beds to balance the cultivated look of his commercial varieties. The most common wayside plants in his garden were white oxeye daisies, crimson corn poppies, yellow flag iris, and wispy oat grasses. He called these plants "the soul of the garden." The oxeye daisies and oat grasses added to the shimmer, and the appearance of diminutive corn poppies and wavy yellow flag irises were like fluttering butterflies. All are part of the formula that made his garden look like a glorious Impressionist painting, composed of flickering brush strokes, especially when viewed from a distance in the muted light of a misty morning.

Above: *Wild oxeye daisies and Siberian wallflowers help offset the highly cultivated look of Monet's flower borders.* **Left:** *A hybrid powderpuff form of herbaceous peony and hybrid bearded irises produce strong clear colors for a beautiful cool color harmony. Monet's liking for hybrids, and his willingness to pay high prices for them, made his garden the most colorful in Europe.*

Chapter Two

MONET'S COLOR HARMONIES

"What I will bring back from here is sweetness itself, white, pink, and blue."

—MONET, ON A TRIP

TO THE MEDITERRANEAN

An informal hot color harmony partners red cottage tulips with yellow Siberian wallflowers and cheerful orange and yellow pansies. The pink stucco cottage in the background is a gardener's residence.

TECHNICALLY, MONET BUILT UP HIS CANVASES WITH A MYRIAD OF BRUSH STROKES, USING MANY COLORS IN JUXTAPOSITION AND RELYING ON THEIR COMBINED EFFECT TO CREATE STUNNINGLY COLORFUL, UPLIFTING IMAGES. FORM WAS PAINTED IN VIEW OF THE ELEMENTS OF LIGHT, NOT WITH THE TRADITIONAL SHARP OUTLINING OF SHAPES. 🐝 GEORGES JEANNIOT, AN ART CRITIC WRITING FOR A POPULAR ART MAGAZINE IN 1888, ANALYZED MONET'S PAINTING STYLE CLOSELY AND REPORTED: "ONCE IN FRONT OF HIS EASEL, HE DRAWS A FEW LINES WITH THE CHARCOAL AND THEN ATTACKS THE PAINTING DIRECTLY, HANDLING HIS LONG BRUSHES WITH AN ASTOUNDING AGILITY AND AN UNERRING SENSE OF DESIGN. HE PAINTS WITH A FULL BRUSH AND USES FOUR OR FIVE PURE COLORS; HE JUXTAPOSES OR SUPERIMPOSES THE UNMIXED COLORS ON THE CANVAS. HIS LANDSCAPE IS QUICKLY SET DOWN AND COULD, IF NECESSARY, BE CONSIDERED COMPLETE AFTER ONLY ONE SESSION, A SESSION WHICH LASTS... AS LONG AS THE EFFECT HE IS SEEKING LASTS, AN HOUR AND OFTEN MUCH LESS. HE IS ALWAYS WORKING ON TWO OR THREE CANVASES AT ONCE: HE BRINGS THEM ALL ALONG, AND PUTS THEM ON THE EASEL AS THE LIGHT CHANGES. THIS IS HIS METHOD."

Oil paints packaged in tubes let artists paint outdoors more easily. These paints were owned by Pierre-Auguste Renoir, Monet's life-long friend, and are on display in the Renoir Museum at Cagnes-sur-Mer.

IMPRESSIONISM AND THE GARDEN

Several changes to artists' materials made painting gardens more attractive to Impressionists than ever, and these changes were in fact contributing factors to the movement itself. Many of these developments involved the way that artists worked with color, and for Monet and other gardeners, some of these innovations affected the way they looked at their gardens, too.

The packaging of oil paints in tubes, a new concept during the era of Impressionism, allowed painters more freedom to work outdoors and to capture fleeting moments of light that could be easily overlooked when painted later in the studio. Around this time, too, heavy metals were added to artists' paints to produce brighter colors.

The invention of photography, which effectively froze a moment in time, also influenced the artists' ability to paint gardens and their willingness to experiment with style. Because a photograph captured every detail, simply rendering a scene realistically was no longer satisfying to many painters. Thus the dimension of exaggeration and feeling came into play in expressing the artist's view of a subject. Also, photography was useful in introducing painters to unusual viewpoints, such as an aerial view of a landscape. Monet, Caillebotte, and Cézanne used photography in varying degrees, and all had darkrooms to do their own processing. For Monet's monumental water lily panels, he most likely used photographs of the water butted together to help determine the best panoramic sequence. A tell-

The Poppies (1873), *painted near Argenteuil, France, shows a stunning red, silver, and green triadic color harmony. Monet admired the color scheme so much that he transferred it to his garden, using cultivated plants such as red geraniums, pink roses with vigorous green leaves, and silver-leaved dianthus to make the display.*

tale photograph shows Monet's image caught in a reflection as he triggered the shutter.

When challenged for painting a view of the Thames from a photograph, Monet flew into a rage at the suggestion that his canvas was any less artistic for his having used a photograph to aid his memory, and declared that the means was irrelevant—he maintained that it was the result that mattered.

Another important influence on Impressionists, including Monet, was the sudden flow of new ideas from Japan. After centuries of isolation, Japan had begun to trade with the West. When Japanese art, pottery, furnishings, and fabrics flooded European cities, painters were exposed to new artistic viewpoints and techniques. Not only were the motifs very different from European tastes, so too were the angles of perspective and framing. The seasonal overtones of much Japanese art gave western painters a better appreciation of nature, especially flowers and gardens for subject matter. Whereas popular European motifs had been romantic landscapes, glorified battles on land and sea, and religious and mythological motifs, the

Japanese motifs were simple, highly animated scenes of earthly and domestic bliss—birds among plum branches, a garden painted in snow, closeups of flowers with butterflies and bees, rock formations, and bridges that formed graceful arcs.

COLOR THEORY

The major force that shaped the Impressionist movement—and extended to the way gardeners then and now combine plants—was the publication of the world's first color wheel by French chemist and physicist Michel-Eugène Chevreul. He showed how colors are changed by the influence of light, an observation that inspired artists to depart from traditional concepts of rendering color. Though Sir Isaac Newton was the first to reveal the colors of daylight with a glass prism, it was Chevreul who proved that all colors are created by mixing the three primary colors, red, blue, and yellow. Chevreul explained how opposites on the color wheel make the best contrasts, and how the combination of two or

PERFECT PARTNERS

MONET DISCOVERED ONE OF HIS FAVORITE COLOR HARMONIES—SILVER, GREEN, AND RED—WHILE PAINTING A FIELD OF POPPIES. THE SILVER IN THIS WILDFLOWER MEADOW COMES FROM DUSTY MILLER (SENECIO MARITIMA), WHILE IN HIS PAINTING THE SILVERY LEAVES BELONG TO WILD SAGE. MONET RE-CREATED THE TRIADIC SILVER-GREEN-RED COMBINATION IN ISLAND BEDS BELOW HIS PORCH, USING BRIGHT RED GERANIUMS AND SILVERY DIANTHUS.

more colors could produce the effect of a separate color when viewed from a distance, as in knitted fabrics.

Color theory was hotly debated among the Impressionists, and several treatises were published on the subject, including two by the garden writers Joseph Decaisne and Claude Naudin. Both Monet and Gertrude Jekyll owned copies of these books. There is also evidence that they learned from each other: Monet was a subscriber to Britain's prestigious *Country Life* magazine, for whom Miss Jekyll wrote a popular gardening column. And he owned copies of her books, though it is not clear whether he acquired these himself or they were sent to him unsolicited.

Monet made good use of the knowledge of color theory he gained from his readings and his discussions with other artists. Since he planted his gardens to paint, he applied his thoughts on color harmonies to the plant combinations he chose.

RED-GREEN-SILVER 〰 Monet discovered a particularly beautiful color combination while painting a field of poppies—the triadic harmony of red, green, and silver. Since silver is not evident on the chromatic wheel, this beautiful color harmony could be fully appreciated only by Monet's discovery of the poppy field and his painting of it, *Poppy Field in Hollow near Giverny* (1885). The red in the painting comes from corn poppies that form a brilliant rectangle almost the size of a football field in a hollow that is very green. On opposite sides of the hollow are drifts of silvery wild sage. Monet transferred this appealing color combination to his garden, using red geraniums in a rectangular bed and silver-leaved dianthus as a prominent edging. Green comes not only from the bold, ruffled leaves of the geraniums, but also from the lustrous green leaves of pink roses planted as standards down the middle of the bed. Add these plants to your garden for an unusual and sophisticated color harmony, or substitute your own favorites in the red, green, and silver color range.

BLUE-PINK-WHITE 〰 A long sojourn near Menton, on the French Riviera, inspired in Monet an appreciation of the blue and pink tones he noted in the landscape. The blue of the sea and sky mixed with the pink of the afternoon sun shining on

Parallel borders in Monet's flower garden present opposing color themes: pink tulips, blue Dutch irises, and a white-flowering crab apple make up a cool spring display, while the facing bed of English wallflowers features a hot color harmony.

hazy white cliffs or white buildings. To make blue and pink planting schemes shine more brilliantly in his garden, Monet combined them with white flowers. For a design reminiscent of Monet's plantings, you might include pink and blue columbine interplanted with white dame's rocket; pink and blue larkspur with white feverfew; or pink coralbells, blue flax, and white chamomile.

YELLOW-VIOLET Opposites on the color wheel, yellow and violet are common color themes in Impressionist paintings. Monet fostered this color combination throughout the seasons, using violet-blue pansies and yellow tulips in spring, yellow African marigolds and violet-blue sage in summer, and yellow sunflowers and violet-blue New England asters in autumn. All are good plant combinations, and will keep your garden interesting in successive seasons. Other possibilities in the yellow and violet color ranges are yellow 'Golden Showers' roses entwined with violet-blue Jackman's clematis and blue morning glories growing among yellow sunflowers.

ORANGE-BLUE Orange and blue, also opposites on the color wheel, is a combination especially effective in summer, when orange flowers abound. For a sensational look, contrast them against a clear blue sky or sparkling blue water. Orange and blue is also a good color harmony for autumn—think fiery orange nasturtiums and vibrant blue morning glories. These two colors create a lovely color harmony when combined with yellow and violet. For other orange and blue combinations, consider orange Mexican sunflowers (*Tithonia rotundifolia*) or orange calendulas and blue pansies.

Above: Violet-blue bicolored bearded irises and bright yellow Siberian wallflowers illustrate Monet's love for the yellow-violet color theme. Opposite: Island beds brimming with white-tipped pink cottage tulips and blue forget-me-nots create one of Monet's favorite color harmonies, blue, pink, and white. To the right is the main house, to the left Monet's second studio. He had another studio in the house and built a third on the opposite side of the house so that he could paint eight huge water lily panels.

 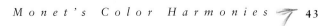

A mass planting of bearded irises shares the color and movement that characterize Impressionist paintings.

SEASONAL DISPLAY IN MONET'S GARDEN

Remembering that Monet planted his gardens to paint gives us a clue about many of his plant choices. Sometimes the effect he wanted to paint was fleeting, and he did not seem to mind that the flower display was painfully short, as other gardeners do. It was necessary for a display to last only long enough to capture on canvas. There are many letters from Monet to friends, urging them to come on a particular day of the week, when he expected the garden to peak. To Caillebotte he writes, "Don't forget to come on Monday, as arranged; all my irises will be in flower, later they will be faded."

After studying an archival photograph of Monet's garden, one observer wondered whatever possessed Monet to plant a particular combination, since the photograph makes the planting appear unfinished and even ugly. The photograph is of an apple orchard with tall sunflowers reaching up among the trees. The bases of the sunflowers are naked, made more hideous by ugly supports. They beg for some color to hide their tall, spindly stems.

PERFECT PARTNERS

ONE STRIKING AND EASY-TO-GROW BLACK AND WHITE COLOR COMBINATION IS HOLLYHOCKS IN WHITE AND SHADES OF BLACK OR DARK MAROON (WHICH OFTEN SERVES AS A "BLACK" IN COLOR COMBINATIONS). MONET USED BLACK VIOLAS LIBERALLY THROUGHOUT HIS GARDEN, ESPECIALLY TO TEMPER THE BRILLIANCE OF RED AND ORANGE FLOWERS. GARDENERS AT GIVERNY TODAY PLANT SIMILAR BLACK AND WHITE MOTIFS IN RECOGNITION OF MONET'S MASTERPIECE *THE MAGPIE*, WHICH SHOWS A BLACK AND WHITE BIRD ON A WATTLE FENCE IN A SNOW-COVERED GARDEN.

Obviously, Monet was interested in painting the yellow sunflower heads in company with orange-red apples against a clear blue sky. The base of the sunflowers would not show in his painting, so why bother planting around them? He was a pragmatist. And he had enough space in his five acres of garden to move on to another area when his painting of one section of the garden was completed.

Monet was so particular about color harmonies in his garden that he even color-coordinated the clothes of people when they appeared in his compositions. In *House at Argenteuil* (1873), a blue and white garden motif is made all the more appealing by two of his stepchildren wearing blue and white dresses. In *Monet's Garden at Giverny* (1895), a woman with red hair wears a straw hat, cream-colored dress, and brown wool sweater—in perfect harmony with the red, orange, and yellow roses. (This fine-tuned coordination was lost on Gertrude Jekyll, who wore only black in her garden.) Monet's own style of dress when touring the garden was earthy brown English tweeds and pastel-colored batiste shirts with pleated cuffs.

Today, the curators of Monet's garden, Mr. and Mrs. Gerald van der Kemp, are aware that visitors do not want to see sections of garden with scraggly bare patches. They want to see color in every season, and the beds are planted intensively so that people strolling along the paths have something colorful always coming into view.

In fact, concern for seasonality and overall view are the main differences between the plantings of Gertrude Jekyll and those of Monet. Jekyll wanted color to flow from one end of a border to the other, with a beginning, a middle, and an end, one color complementing the next, and repeating. Since Monet looked to his garden for particular motifs, he often had in mind a specific position to set his easel and execute the painting and therefore planted self-contained areas rather than complete beds.

COOL COLORS—SUNRISE BORDERS

Because of Monet's desire to paint his garden, he seems to have developed a very refined appreciation of the relationship between the colors of plants at different times of the day

PERFECT PARTNERS

THE DRAMA OF RED AND GREEN IS EVIDENT IN THIS PLANTING OF RED ROSES AND BRONZE JAPANESE MAPLES IN COMPANY WITH A RICH TAPESTRY OF FOLIAGE. THE LEAF SHAPES, INCLUDING THE WHISPY BLADES OF DAYLILIES AND THE LARGE SERRATED FOLIAGE OF GIANT HOG WEED, CONTRIBUTE ADDITIONAL INTEREST TO THE SCHEME. THIS IS PART OF THE GIVERNY GARDEN OF ARTIST JEAN-MARIE TOULGOUAT, WHO IS DESCENDED FROM THE MARRIAGE OF BLANCHE MONET TO THE AMERICAN IMPRESSIONIST PAINTER THEODORE BUTLER.

and under different lighting conditions. For example, the beds on the east side of Monet's garden were dominated by cool colors: light pink, purple, mauve, and pale yellow. The cool light of the rising sun sharpened these colors, producing a beautifully soothing effect. These are his "sunrise" borders.

When planted in shade, sunrise colors are the first to disappear in dwindling light. But on a sunny day, or even on a high overcast day, cool colors—especially blue, purple, and mauve—look sensational in shade, appearing to glow softly in the dimness.

Observe your garden throughout the day to gain an appreciation of the quality of light at different times. Choose plants for your various beds and borders based on when you are most likely to spend time there. For instance, if the garden surrounding your patio faces the rising sun and you like to have coffee there in the early morning, plant a sunrise border with flowers in cool shades of pale pink, purple, and yellow. Bearded irises, pansies, and tulips all provide these soft colors, or substitute your own favorite pastel flowers.

HOT COLORS—SUNSET BORDERS

On the west side of his flower garden Monet planted hot colors—bright yellow, orange, and scarlet—which were intensified by the warm rays of the setting sun. Flowers in hot colors are absolutely brilliant positioned in sunny spots.

A wonderful description of a hot color planting is given to us by novelist and art critic Octave Mirbeau following a visit to Monet's garden in the spring:

> Nasturtiums of all colors and saffron-colored eschscholzias collapse in blinding ruins on both sides of the sandy pathway. In the wide flower beds, covering the irises stripped of their blossoms, surges the surprising magic of the poppies, an extraordinary mixture of

Opposite: *Monet's "sunrise" borders (designed to look their best in early-morning light) are composed mainly of the blue tones of bearded irises. Scattered white peonies and the snowy highlights of bicolored irises create a glittering sensation that enhances the intensity of the blues.*

PERFECT PARTNERS

For shady areas, the gardeners at Giverny today like to use blue forget-me-nots in company with pink English daisies. This pathside planting enhances the approach to Monet's water garden. A similar effect can be achieved with shade-loving blue and pink pansies.

tones, an orgy of bright nuances, a resplendent and musical muddle of white, pink, yellow and mauve; an unbelievable kneading of blond flesh tones, on which the orange tones burst, the fanfares of burning copper ring out, the reds bleed and catch fire, the violet tones brighten, and the dark crimsons light up.

Determine the area of your garden that receives the fiery light of the setting sun and plant accordingly. Make sure to plan your sunset border so that you can fully appreciate it. Set two chairs or a bench so that they face both the planting and the setting sun, and start a tradition of evening drinks or after-dinner coffee there. Perhaps you'll want to create an outdoor dining area where the family can enjoy evening meals bathed in the warm light of the sinking sun.

HAZY EFFECTS AND THE ILLUSION OF DISTANCE

Monet was careful about placing colors in his garden, positioning hot-colored flowers in the foreground and pale or pastel flowers behind them. Since hot colors tend to "advance" and cool colors to "recede," Monet's carefully calculated placements created the illusion of greater distance. You can use these concepts to increase the visual distance in your own garden; this technique is especially useful in small gardens, where the impression of depth created by a well-orchestrated planting of flowers in hot and cool colors is particularly welcome. Any of your favorite flowers in shades of red, bright yellow, and orange will serve admirably in hot

color roles—English wallflowers were among those best-loved by Monet. For the cool colors, choose flowers in pale pink, blue, and purple, such as bearded irises and New England asters, which were some of Monet's favorites.

The pale flowers Monet planted in the background also contributed a hazy effect—this impression of haze can be amplified by using flowering plants with misty-looking flowers. These include lavender (especially the pale blue kind), tamarix (with misty pink blossoms), and smoke bush (with misty pink or white blossoms).

Above: *Lavender produces a hazy effect along one of* Monet's *plante bands in the* Clos Normand *flower garden.* **Opposite:** *A "sunset" border, best viewed against the light of the sinking sun, uses yellow, orange, and red* English wallflowers. *The outstretched arms of a crab apple add structural interest and tie the hot color border to the* Clematis montana *climbing high on a trellis.*

Chapter Three

MONET'S FAVORITE STRUCTURES

"You enter the aquatic garden over a hog-backed bridge covered with wisteria. In June the fragrance is so heavy that it is like going through a tunnel of vanilla. The clusters, light and mauve, a light mauve that one would say was painted in watercolor, fall like fanciful grapes in the watery greenery of the creepers. The passing breeze harvests the aroma."

—OCTAVE MIRBEAU, ART CRITIC

Monet's famous benches can each seat six people. Here, the benches face each other, ornamented by a planting of yellow trumpet daffodils in the shade of a flowering cherry.

MONET HAD VERY DEFINITE LIKES AND DISLIKES CONCERNING ORNAMENTS IN THE GARDEN, AND AVOIDED ANYTHING CONTRIVED OR OSTENTATIOUS. ACCORDING TO HIS STEPSON, HE DISLIKED "ROCKS WITH CASCADES, GIANT CEMENT MUSHROOMS, COLUMNS, STATUES, TOPIARY, VICTORIAN BEDDING...." BUT HE DID SHARE THE IMPRESSIONISTS' LOVE OF BENCHES. HE USED THEM NOT ONLY AS GOOD PLACES FROM WHICH TO VIEW THE GARDEN, BUT ALSO AS FINE ACCENTS IN THE OVERALL PLAN. HE USED OTHER STRUCTURES MAINLY TO GROW PLANTS UPON, AND PARTICULARLY LIKED ARBORS AND TRELLISES, WHICH EXTENDED COLOR HIGH INTO THE SKY.

BENCHES

Monet had several kinds of slatted benches in his Clos Normand flower garden. The most conspicuous is a six-seater with a curved seat and backrest. This bench has been

Monet discovered the prototype for his curved, slatted benches on the grounds of Versailles Palace, where the original bench can be found even today.

reproduced worldwide, and is sold commercially, even through mail-order catalogs. The catalogs invariably describe the bench as an original Monet design. Actually, the original design can be found today on the grounds of Versailles, where Monet went several times to paint with Renoir. The bench is located in an area known as Le Petit Hameau, a quaint village of cottages and a snuff mill, where Marie Antoinette escaped from the formality of court life. The bench at Versailles sits snugly beneath a rose-covered balcony with a commanding view of a water lily pond, not unlike the lily pond Monet later established at Giverny. The Versailles bench is unpainted, but when Monet made replicas of it for his own garden, he painted them apple green to match the shutters of his house. Adding a bench in a classic design, or even a simple garden seat, will do much to enhance your garden with simple ornament and to create a serene viewing place. Paint the bench in a color that matches the trim of your own house, or perhaps in a shade that matches your planting scheme, to re-create the understated beauty of Monet's garden.

In another part of the water garden, Monet placed curved stone benches of Oriental design within a thicket of bamboo. These benches form a semicircle, or exedra, around a beautiful old beech tree underplanted with daffodils. The exedra is an arrangement that allows a group of people to sit facing each other, promoting intimate discussion. Monet may have adopted this garden element after visiting Caillebotte's family estate at Yerres, which also features an exedra. If you have the space for a series of benches, consider buying curved pieces and positioning them as an exedra—you'll be surprised how often you and your guests will gravitate to this pleasant spot for relaxed conversation. Make sure to plant the area surrounding the bench so that conversation is not the only draw. Like any other garden bench, it should also be a place where the view can be appreciated.

BOATS

An often overlooked feature of Monet's water garden is a green and black flat-bottomed rowboat, used by the gardeners for clearing the pond surface of algae. Monet painted its sleek lines often, and allowed it to drift out into the pond at the end of a rope. The boat was a beautiful embellishment to the pond, though today it is more likely to be found pulled up onto the bank and hidden among bamboo to discourage visitors to the garden from using it. If your property includes a lake or pond, don't feel that you have to hide your boats. Instead, celebrate their clean, simple lines and add the dimension of gentle movement by giving them enough rope to drift, just as Monet did.

Beside his stone boat dock Monet placed a slatted wooden bench. The bench and dock

Top: *A pair of stone benches in Monet's water garden forms an exedra. The curved seats are backed by an immense grove of bamboo, which forms a semicircle and arching tunnel.* **Above:** *Monet's rowboat is used by the gardeners to clear the pond of algae and maintain a separation between the islands of water lilies. It is also a beautiful landscape feature, often painted by Monet with and without people.*

served as an observation platform from which he could view the reflections on the water. The bench and boat dock remain, and are still partially overhung with arches of rambling roses.

There is a marvelous view of the boat dock in Monet's painting *The Flowering Arches* (1913); exquisite water reflections cause the rose arches to form a complete circle of color around the boat dock.

BRIDGES

Bridges are the other prominent structures in Monet's water garden. One, which Monet called the Japanese bridge, spans a stream flowing from his water lily pond. Featuring a high arch, it was originally painted white to conspicuously reflect in the water. The white paint picked up colors from the light and sur-

Above: This approach to Monet's boat dock is arched over with climbing roses, and features a slatted bench where the painter loved to sit and admire the pond. **Right:** *Fragrant 'Exbury' hybrid azaleas are framed by the distant branches of wisteria. Trained across a canopy above the bridge, the white wisteria is a perfect foil for the bright coral azaleas.* **Opposite: The Water Lily Pond (1899),** *depicts Monet's Japanese bridge before he built the canopy over it. The positioning of the bridge in a prominent arc across the canvas and the carpet of water lilies on the pond's surface produce a telephoto effect that may have been inspired by Monet's familiarity with photography.*

Wisteria in two colors, white and mauve-blue, intertwine above the Japanese-style bridge in Monet's water garden. The swirling tracery of branches overhead is supported by a sturdy metal frame, while the lush blooms cascade over the sides of the canopy.

stream is planted luxuriously all along its length with flowering cherries and colonies of perennial plants like daylilies and hostas.

When Monet first started painting his water garden the bridge was his favorite motif. *Water Lily Pond* (1899) shows the water lilies gathered together in the foreground and the bridge bleeding off the edges of the canvas in an effect similar to that of a photograph taken with a telephoto lens.

Later, when Monet realized the beauty of the reflections on his pond, his viewpoint changed from looking across the pond to looking directly down on it, even excluding the pond shore, as in *Water Lilies* (1905). His career culminated with a series of eight spectacular horizontal panels that butt together to create a continuous panorama. Again, it is the reflections that are the focus of this set of immense paintings—Monet captures flawlessly the quality of light on the water, ranging from areas that are dark and sinister to bright, uplifting sections that reflect cream-colored clouds and an azure sky.

Not many gardeners have the luxury of a stream flowing through their gardens. If

rounding plants—orange and apricot at sunset and green from surrounding foliage when the light was more muted. Later Monet painted the entire bridge green, added a canopy, and threaded the canopy with wisteria, creating a spectacular effect when the white and mauve wisteria bloomed. The gardens also featured several other small, flat, or slightly arched footbridges painted green and white. These cross a water inlet and crisscross parts of a stream that bypasses the pond, so that a stroll through the water garden does not involve merely a walk around the pond, but extends to parts of the garden that incorporate a fast-running stream. The

you are one of the lucky ones, consider building an arching footbridge at a strategic point. Though only still water offers the stunning reflections Monet so loved to paint, the bridge itself will contribute a picturesque quality reminiscent of the gardens at Giverny. Plant the streambanks with yellow and blue flag irises, pink swamp mallow, and red cardinal flowers. If your stream is wide and extremely slow moving, or if you have a narrow pond across which to build your bridge, you may even capture some of the same sorts of reflections on which Monet based many of his paintings.

ARBORS

In addition to high arches grouped around the boat dock, Monet built a long, sleek arbor to support a blue-flowering wisteria vine. The arbor arches out over a path of beige-colored gravel, coloring it briefly in late spring with fallen mauve-blue petals. During the first week of May, this stretch of wisteria appears as a long brush stroke of color when observed from the opposite bank.

Including an arbor in your garden lends an instant aura of romance to the space. If you plan to copy Monet and plant your arbor with wisteria, make sure that you construct an extremely sturdy one. Wisteria is a very heavy, woody vine, and requires strong support. If you'd rather not worry about your arbor's structural integrity, plant lighter vines like clematis, the perennial silver fleece vine (*Polygonum aubertii*) and the annual firecracker vine (*Mina lobata*), which will provide plenty of color and still add a simple elegance to the garden.

A simple straight arbor creates a brush stroke of blue at the edge of the pond at Giverny. As the wisteria flowers fade, the falling petals color the path like confetti.

PERFECT PARTNERS

A STRONG METAL FRAME SUPPORTS AN OLD WISTERIA VINE MONET PLANTED BETWEEN THE PATH AND HIS POND; THE WISTERIA CARRIES COLOR HIGH INTO THE OVERHEAD LEAF CANOPY, MINGLING ITS SPLASHES OF BLUE WITH THE WHITE OF A CHESTNUT IN THE BACKGROUND. THIS PAIRING OF WISTERIA AND CHESTNUT PRESENTS A BEAUTIFUL TUNNEL EFFECT, MAKING EVERY TURN ALONG THE PATH A VISUAL ADVENTURE.

GATES

There is a substantial gate at the entrance to Monet's water garden, which bears a crisscross design similar to a pattern used by Caillebotte in his garden. Garden gates can be an important structural feature, lending support to vines and climbers, serving as a definitive entrance to the garden, marking the division between separate gardens, and providing punctuation to the winter garden. Your gate need not be an opening in a wall or fence, though this is the traditional arrangement. Let the gate stand at a break in a hedge or with tall plants on either side, creating a sort of natural fence.

THE GRANDE ALLÉE—A FLORAL TUNNEL

The most impressive structure that Monet created for his property is undoubtedly the Grande Allée—a series of six arched metal spans that vault a wide path leading from the main door of the house to the back gate. The arches are covered with climbing roses that bloom for most of summer and the path is festooned with nasturtiums as well. Parallel raised beds, planted with an assortment of annuals, perennials, and flowering bulbs form the sides of the tunnel.

More than anything else in the garden, the Grande Allée is unique. The more common leaf tunnels, usually formed from hedges of hornbeam or beech so the branches meet overhead, had long been a feature of French gardens. Cézanne's garden at Aix-en-Provence is full of such leaf tunnels.

Monet's originality in creating a true floral tunnel, with nasturtiums almost knitting together from opposite ends of the path, is ingenious. The secret of Monet's nasturtium path is revealed in his painting *The Artist's Garden at Vétheuil* (1880), which depicts his hillside garden at Vétheuil, where he lived before moving to Giverny. The painting is a hot color harmony, dominated by spires of red gladiolus and yellow sunflowers. It shows a flight of steep steps leading down into the garden, with orange nasturtiums creeping across the treads from opposite sides, completing a dramatic orange-red-yellow scheme. Moreover, this use of nasturtiums to decorate a flight of steps has long been a popular planting scheme in both the South of

Above: *Monet's Grand Allée in early autumn shows its six massive metal rose arches. Nasturtiums creep across the path, backed by late-blooming New England asters and perennial sunflowers.* **Opposite: Artist's Garden at Vétheuil (1881)** *captures a stunning hot color harmony yellow sunflowers, orange nasturtiums creeping in from both sides of the steps, and red gladiolus in Oriental pots. The blue of the sky and of the pot design are a stunning contrast for the warm floral colors.*

PERFECT PARTNERS

ESPALIERED PEAR TREES AND A COLLECTION OF VINES, INCLUDING YELLOW-FLOWERING *CLEMATIS TANGUTICA* AND RED-FOLIAGED VIRGINIA CREEPER, COVER A DIAMOND-SHAPED TRELLIS. THE BUILDING BEYOND THE WALL IS NOW PART OF THE MONET FOUNDATION, AND IS USED AS HOUSING FOR ART STUDENTS.

France and North Africa, where Monet had traveled. Though the transition from a steep flight of steps to a flat, broad path was a natural progression from the common interpretation of the planting, the Grande Allée's overall design, using climbing roses to complete the flowering tunnel effect, is undoubtedly unique.

TRELLISES

Monet's Clos Normand was enclosed by a high stone wall capped with clay tiles. He reduced its height along the bottom of his property to gain a view of the neighboring countryside, and added a wrought-iron fence to the top of the lowered wall, along which he trained vines. The other walls he covered with a green, crisscrossing wooden trellis, on which he grew an assortment of espaliered trees.

A good example of Monet's trelliswork appears in his painting *Gladioli* (1876), in which the diamond pattern of a trellis breaks up a monotonous expanse of wall. Like Monet, you can add subtle pattern along with the color and greenery of vines by adding a trellis to your garden. Along a solid wall or on the side of a house, a trellis can be an effective accent. Plant it with fast-growing vines like morning glories and nasturtiums for instant gratification, or enjoy the slow progress of perennial vines such as honeysuckle, climbing roses, and Virginia creeper.

PLANTERS

Many of Monet's paintings feature planters. The beauty of growing flowers in planters is that they may be moved around and placed wherever they will most effectively complement a composition. Monet used blue and white barrel-shaped planters in an Oriental willow pattern to display gladiolus. He also used square wooden boxes to show off the lush, bushy forms of fuchsias covered with red and pink pendant blooms.

Opposite: *Blue and white oriental planters act as sentinels beside the steps leading from Monet's porch into the garden. The pots hold forsythia trained as standards, an unusual treatment for this early-spring favorite.*

Monet's boxes were small versions of the ever-popular Versailles planter. Originally used at the Palace of Versailles to hold palm trees and orange trees, these square wooden planters were placed on casters so that the trees could be easily moved indoors during winter.

Containers are an excellent way to experiment with plants without investing too much time and effort. As the gardeners at Versailles noted, containers can also be moved indoors to protect tender plants when cold weather arrives, allowing you to plant species that you otherwise couldn't grow. Another bonus: if the plants seem to be failing because of their situation (too much or too little light, a location not sheltered enough, etc.), the problem can be remedied by simply moving the container. You can also reposition your containers throughout the year to take advantage of their peak bloom time, placing them in the spotlight when they look their best and letting them recede into the background when they are upstaged by another plant combination.

GREENHOUSES

Monet's greenhouse was strictly functional. Although it could have been made more ornamental, like the Victorian greenhouses that featured arched window frames and roof finials, Monet chose not to give it any special architectural significance. Impressed with a greenhouse installed on Caillebotte's property, Monet built his along similar lines, consulting with the director of the Jardin des Plantes, where several state-of-the-art greenhouses for growing tropical plants had been constructed. Monet's greenhouse was, in fact, a commercial-style greenhouse popular at the time in Holland for growing carnations and other florist flowers. Monet used his greenhouse for growing orchids, exotic chrysanthemums, tropical water lilies, and angel-wing begonias, and for the propagation of seeds and cuttings. The greenhouse was located along the west wall of his Clos Normand, surrounded by cold frames for hardening off seedlings.

PERFECT PARTNERS

BIRDS AND BUTTERFLIES WERE IMPORTANT TO MONET'S PERCEPTION OF THE PERFECT GARDEN, AND WILL BRING VIBRANT LIFE TO YOUR OWN GARDEN. FOR MONET, BUTTERFLIES PROVIDED THE FLICKERING MOVEMENT HE LIKED TO CAPTURE ON CANVAS; BIRDS ADDED MUSIC TO THE ATMOSPHERE AS HE PAINTED. ORIENTAL-STYLE BIRD FEEDERS AND NESTING BOXES ARE STRATEGICALLY PLACED THROUGHOUT THE GARDEN, HERE AMONG LABURNUMS—THEIR TRUNKS PRUNED BARE OF LOWER BRANCHES TO ACCENTUATE THEIR SINUOUS LINES—IN THE WATER GARDEN.

A neighbor, Lilla Cabot Perry, recalls that when the heating system was installed, Monet fretted over its efficiency. To satisfy his concern, he decided to sleep in the greenhouse overnight. When his wife and the rest of the family heard about this they all wanted to sleep in the greenhouse, and did, like a group of happy campers. The heating system worked fine.

Apart from a spacious canopied porch running almost the length of the structure, there is little other form of ornamentation—no sundials, statuary, balustrades, fountains, lanterns, or any other form of decoration that might detract from the beauty of the plants.

To repeat Monet's greenhouse style, keep your greenhouse as simple as possible, remembering that to him it was purely a functional space. A classic structure of glass is a good option and will allow you to overwinter your plants, grow exotics, and start seedlings early. Note that you can perform these tasks inside your home if a greenhouse doesn't fit your space or budget.

Monet's greenhouse is almost hidden by trees in this view from the bottom of the garden, looking up toward the second studio. Note the pronounced lines of perspective formed by parallel paths and straight flower borders, which look rather stark in early spring but are softened by luxuriant growth in summer.

Chapter Four

THE WATER GARDEN

"A landscape doesn't get under your skin in one day. And then all of a sudden I had the revelation of how enchanting my pond was. I took up my palette. Since then I've had hardly any other subject."

—MONET, ON HIS WATER GARDEN

Water irises of many kinds are important pondside accents, contrasting their stiff, spiky foliage with the softness of weeping willows. Here, the wild European flag iris (*Iris pseudacorus*) partners a clump of coral-colored azaleas and a purple-leafed Japanese maple in early spring.

To describe Monet's magnificent water garden as a Japanese garden is not completely accurate. Indeed, when a visiting Japanese diplomat complimented Monet on his success at creating a Japanese garden, Monet replied that the similarity was unintentional. Though the two are similar in feeling, an authentic Japanese garden includes many elements missing from Monet's design. A Japanese water garden invariably features stone structures such as massive boulder formations, flagstone walks, and stepping stones, plus artificially weathered tree forms. The water garden's Japanese atmosphere arose out of Monet's keen understanding of the Japanese garden design aesthetic; but he selected from the Japanese tradition only those elements that appealed to his artistic sensibilities. He installed the high-arched bridge after admiring a similar bridge in a Japanese woodblock print, and he even hired a Japanese horticulturist to help him choose plants, such as tree peonies, hardy species of bamboo, Japanese primulas, hostas, Japanese irises, and Japanese butterbur. The meandering path, too, is typical of Japanese stroll gardens. It twists and turns in hairpin bends into neighboring shrubby areas, making maximum use of a confined space. The path completely encircles the pond, with strategic observation points along its length. The result is a garden with a distinctly Japanese appearance. But it is uniquely Monet's work of art, as different from traditional Japanese gardens as Impressionism is from Japanese silkscreen art. Conspicuously absent from Monet's water garden are the stone lanterns, rocky cascades, severely pruned pines, azaleas clipped into globular shapes, and tea houses that help define a Japanese garden. In his own garden, Monet achieved a design much more natural than the highly stylized, traditional Japanese garden.

Monet was greatly aided in his understanding of Japanese art and garden design by his neighbor Lilla Cabot Perry. Her husband's great-uncle was Commodore Perry, who opened Japan to the West. As a result of the family's Japanese connections, Mrs. Perry's husband was offered a teaching position in Tokyo and for three years the Perrys immersed themselves in Japanese culture and tradition before returning to their Giverny house.

The scheme of the water garden—with its emphasis on water and shadowy foliage effects—is in muted contrast to the glorious organized chaos of the flowery, sunlit Clos Normand. By nature cool and serene, water gardens are perfect counterpoints to the brilliance of flower gardens, and even a small pool can provide a restful note in your landscape. If you haven't the space or the energy for a full-scale water garden, consider trying a few aquatic plants in a container.

Adding a canopy to the Japanese bridge allowed color to become an element on a more elevated level. In spring, the bridge is alight with the white and mauve blooms of wisteria.

WISTERIA

Monet would frequently drop in to see his friends the Perrys after his midday meal, with gardening and Japan the main topics of conversation. He had a special admiration for Mrs. Perry, for she was not only an accomplished artist, but also highly intelligent. Mrs. Perry even helped Monet with his water garden plantings. She may have described the Sento Imperial Palace Garden, with its magnificent stone bridge and canopy of wisteria, since it was shortly after her return to Giverny that Monet installed the canopy over his own bridge.

The Sento Imperial Palace Garden bridge is flat and its rustic wooden canopy is likewise flat. Monet's bridge was already arched, so an arched canopy suited it better than a flat one

PERFECT PARTNERS

FROTHY PINK FLOWERS OF MEADOW RUE (*THALICTRUM AQUILEGIFOLIUM*) CONTRAST WITH CURTAINS OF WEEPING WILLOW LEAVES BESIDE MONET'S POND IN A SIMPLE JUXTAPOSITION OF COLOR AND FORM. FROM A VISITOR'S DESCRIPTION OF THE WATER GARDEN WE KNOW THAT MONET USED MORE MEADOWSWEET PLANTS THAN ARE EVIDENT IN THE GARDEN TODAY.

would have. He threaded the canopy with two kinds of wisteria—mauve and white, which blooms a bit later, though there is a brief overlapping of bloom. Whether blooming separately or together, the wisteria creates a magnificent effect. A second stretch of wisteria is planted along the stroll path atop a high, metal trellis, as a counterpoint to the wisteria on the bridge. Its branches arch over the path and briefly carpet the ground with fallen petals.

THE CUP GARDEN CONCEPT

In the lexicon of Japanese garden design, Monet's water garden is a cup garden, a design that encourages introspection. The mirror-smooth water forms the bottom of the cup, and the pondside plantings—including weeping willows, thickets of bamboo, and rhododendron—form its sides. The gravel path encircling the pond offers a clear, continuous view of the pond surface—the eye is irresistibly drawn to the water, with its floating islands of water lilies and exquisite reflections. In 1927 François Thiebault Sisson wrote, "In the pond he had planted literally thousands of water lilies, rare and choice varieties of every color of the prism, from violet, red, and orange to pink, lilac, and mauve." In a rare explanation of his water garden, Monet noted, "The effect varies constantly, not only from one season to the next, but from one minute to the next, since the water lilies are far from being the whole scene; really they are just the accompaniment. The essence of the motif is the mirror of water whose appearance alters at every moment, thanks to the patches of sky that are reflected in it, and which give it its light and movement."

The most enchanting aspect of this space is its otherworldly quality. Though located just yards from the Clos Normand, the two gardens are obviously born of different cultures, different

Opposite: *This view of Monet's water garden in summer highlights the beautifully reflective pond surface and the stroll path, which leads through pondside plants.*

worlds. The Clos Normand is Monet's response to the English style of cottage gardening, which he learned to love while visiting that country. It is bright and sunny, exuberant with color—a virtual battle of flowers, with every plant vying for attention. The flower garden slopes downhill, and the pink stucco house dominates the space like a ship in a romantic harbor, its green shutters echoing the verdure of the garden and connecting the house to it.

In contrast, the water garden is almost hidden from view. Its thick stands of shade trees seem to insulate it from all the troubles of the world. While stepping into the water garden is like stepping into a Japanese landscape, absent from the design is the traditional philosophy and symbolism found in Japanese gardens. The water garden is a world created uniquely by Monet, arguably his greatest artistic endeavor and perhaps the world's finest work of art, despite its ephemeral nature.

PERFECT PARTNERS

A HOT COLOR PAIRING OF YELLOW AND ORANGE WALLFLOWERS LIGHTS UP THE STREAMBANK NEAR THE FLAT SPAN THAT LEADS TO MONET'S BOAT DOCK. IN ADDITION TO THE LARGE ARCHED JAPANESE FOOTBRIDGE, WHICH IS THE MAIN FOCAL POINT IN MONET'S WATER GARDEN, THERE ARE SEVERAL OTHER SMALLER FOOTBRIDGES THAT CRISS-CROSS A NEARBY STREAM. ALSO EVIDENT IN THIS PLANTING SCHEME IS THE CON-TRAST OF LIGHT AND SHADOW THAT MONET SO LOVED TO PAINT.

THE TAPESTRY GARDEN—
FOLIAGE EFFECTS

In the Clos Normand one hears the chatter of excited tourists; in the water garden, by contrast, there is nearly always a reverent silence. People speak in whispers, as if in a cathedral. There is no garishness in the water garden; although there are pools of color, they are greatly subdued. Here, foliage effects take prece-

dence. The colors, textures, and shapes of leaves combine in a tapestry of refined contrasts. Slender, curtainlike branches of willow drape beside swirling leaves of Japanese butterbur; lustrous dark green leaves of billowing rhododendrons mingle with the fleecelike shape and lacy leaves of Japanese maples. Fountain grasses and sword-shaped Japanese irises strike through the paddle-shaped leaves of hostas and the cascading straplike leaves of agapanthus. Admittedly, the effect was even more subtle in

Foliage effects from strong greens and purple take precedence over floral color in Monet's water garden. The rich contrast of tree shapes, textures, and colors adds strong decorative appeal to the landscape even when the wisteria canopy is not in bloom.

Monet's day, when he used many mosslike groundcovers. But even today, with gardeners who tend to plant the pondsides with more color than Monet might have permitted, the water garden remains a peaceful, contemplative space.

THE STROLL

Like the emperors of imperial Japan, Monet enjoyed showing off his water garden to visiting dignitaries and close friends, strolling along the path, naming his plants and offering cuttings and growing tips, but largely staying close-lipped about his actual design philosophy. Visitors were forced to extrapolate on Monet's thoughts based on what they knew of him and what they saw in the landscape. One observer noted, "Around the pond he had laid out paths arched with trellises of greenery, paths that twisted and intercrossed to give the illusion of a vast park." A fast-running stream is crossed several times by bridges; the entire length of the streambanks is planted with a rich assortment of flowering and foliage plants.

Opposite: The path twists and winds around the pond, with visual treats all along its length. In early spring, these 'Professor Einstein' daffodils begin to spill into the path. Coral-colored azaleas and 'Barnhaven' primroses edge the path in the distance.

PERFECT PARTNERS

THE FLEECELIKE LIMBS OF A JAPANESE MAPLE AND GRACEFUL, FLOWING BRANCHES OF A WEEPING WILLOW SOFTEN THE DRAMA OF A HOT COLOR HARMONY ALONG A PATH BESIDE MONET'S POND. 'EXBURY' AZALEAS AND CHEERFUL 'BARNHAVEN' PRIMROSES LEND THEIR BRIGHT REDS, ORANGES, AND YELLOWS TO THE SCHEME. COUNTERPOINTS LIKE THE SOOTHING GREEN OF LEAFY TREES SET OFF DYNAMIC PLANTING THEMES PARTICULARLY WELL, MAKING THE HOT COLORS APPEAR ALL THE BRIGHTER.

The Water Lilies

The water lilies, in many shades of pink, red, orange, and yellow plus fragrant whites, are the crowning glory of Monet's water garden. All are hybrids; each began life in the historic village of Temple-sur-Lot, an agricultural community nestled among rolling hills in a plum-growing region four hundred miles (600 kilometers) south of Giverny. With a knowledge of genetics gained from growing and breeding plums,

Joseph Bory Latour-Marliac began a breeding program to improve water lilies. At the time Europeans knew only white waterlilies, but Latour-Marliac found a mutation in Sweden that opened pink and turned red with age. A fragrant white species with a pink mutation grew on Cape Cod. Marliac obtained a yellow from Mexico, and with this gene pool he was able to develop sixty distinct hardy water lily hybrids. An interesting point about Marliac's varieties is that he released only sterile hybrids. This meant that they could not be repro-

Left, top: `Escarboucle` *(the name means carbuncle in French) is a deep carmine-red water lily with a prominent crown of yellow stamens and lustrous, leathery green foliage.* **Left, bottom:** `Chromatella`*, a clear yellow water lily, is featured in many of Monet's paintings. Wherever a yellow water lily appears, it is almost certainly* `Chromatella`*.* **Above:** *The decorative ponds at the Latour-Marliac nursery, where Monet purchased his famous water lilies, have dividers separating different varieties; the shallow terra-cotta pots are used to grow a single variety of water lily.*

Above Left: *Water reflections are most noticeable from a high elevation. The arch of Monet's bridge is a perfect place to appreciate the wonderful reflective quality of the pond, which changes not only from season to season, but from minute to minute as the cloud formations, light, and weather conditions change.* **Above Right:** *Monet repeatedly painted this composition—an island of water lilies framed by the silhouetted branches of a weeping willow from the pondside footpath.*

duced from seed, which produces variable results in water lilies. The only method of propagation was by division, ensuring an identical match with the mother plants.

At various times Monet grew most of Marliac's hybrids: rosy red 'Attraction', bright yellow 'Chromatella', orange 'Comanche', and soft pink 'Caroliniana'. And others, including 'Atropurpurea', 'James Brydon', and 'William Falconer', are also listed on an early invoice. Monet purchased other water and bog-loving plants from the Latour-Marliac nursery. One invoice lists parrot's feather, arrowhead, pickerel weed, bog marigolds, water chestnut, purple loosestrife, and two species of sedge grass. Monet ordered three of everything. The nursery survives to this day much as it did when Marliac and Monet were alive. Indeed, visiting the site is like stepping back in time a hundred years.

Monet cherished Marliac's water lilies, and he nurtured them like no one else in Europe. He planted them in deep, wide containers so the aggressive roots would not run rampant, and so the soil around their roots could be efficiently fertilized to maintain heavy bloom throughout summer. To provide the density of leaves that Monet required he placed as many as three plants in a 25-gallon (95-liter) container, and even more in large containers.

Hybridizing is still carried on, and the Latour-Marliac nursery conducts a lively mail-order business with a colorful catalog that seems little changed over the years. The new owners are a husband-and-wife team, Barbara and Bill Davies. The couple also owns Stapeley Water Gardens, near Chester, England. Several years ago they won a gold medal for their interpretation of a Monet water garden design at the Chelsea Flower Show. Barbara and Bill were extremely helpful to me in researching this book, including locating invoices for me dating to 1894, from the nursery to Monet.

A small-space Monet-style water garden is relatively easy to install in your own garden, using a flexible waterproof liner to seal the bottom of the pool. A kidney shape—approximately 8

PERFECT PARTNERS

YELLOW BROOM AND RED FLOWERING CURRANT ARCH THEIR BRANCHES OUT OVER EXQUISITE TREE REFLECTIONS ON MONET'S POND IN EARLY SPRING. NOTE THAT THE TWIGGY GROWTH OF THE SHRUBS AND THE BRANCHES OF REFLECTING TREES CREATE A TRACERY OF APPEALING SILHOUETTED LINES, REMINISCENT OF AN ARTIST'S SKETCH. IN PAINTINGS OF HIS WATER GARDEN, MONET PARTICULARLY LIKED TO COMBINE REFLECTIONS IN THE WATER WITH ELEMENTS ON THE STREAM BANK TO CREATE UNCONVENTIONAL MOTIFS THAT MADE PEOPLE LOOK HARD TO INTERPRET THE COMPOSITION.

by 12 feet (2.5 by 3.5m)—is sufficient to accommodate several submerged tubs of water lilies, particularly if the varieties are miniatures, such as yellow 'Helvola'. Just remember to separate the tubs of water lilies with enough space so that there is sufficient water surface between the islands of leaves to produce a reflection.

Other water plants can be grown in submerged pots to complement the water lily foliage, the plants strategically positioned around the rim of the pool. Particularly appealing for their leaf shapes are arrowhead plants, cattails, Japanese water irises, yellow flag irises, and papyrus. Around the pool's edge, plant hostas and ferns for more appealing foliage contrasts. A Japanese cutleaf maple and an azalea or two can be encouraged to spread their branches forward to touch the water.

REFLECTIONS IN WATER

To maintain a reflective quality between the islands of foliage, Monet employed a gardener whose sole occupation was to keep the pond clean and maintain a distinct separation between the water lily varieties. Algae was raked from the surface daily, and each island of leaves was regularly trimmed to prevent its mingling with a neighbor.

Toward the end of his life, Monet's only motif was his water lilies. In many of his canvases they seem to float in space,

Even on a rainy day, Monet's pond surface has exquisite slate-gray reflections. The boat, tethered to the side of the pond, provides an important ornamental landscape accent.

since he rarely painted a horizon line or showed the banks of the pond. He painted on sunny days and cloudy days, at morning, noon, and late afternoon, and from every vantage point. This obsession culminated in the masterpiece known as the water lily panels. Today these immense horizontal canvases occupy the walls of two circular rooms in the Orangerie muse-

Monet often painted his water reflections without any horizon line, giving them a mysterious quality. Here, fragrant orange and red 'Exbury' hybrid azaleas produce the kind of reflection that Monet liked to capture on canvas.

um in Paris. The paintings show the surface of the pond at different times of the day, and they required the construction of a special studio to paint. Today, at Giverny, the water lily studio is a spacious gift shop always thronging with visitors.

A testimony to the genius of Marliac's skill as a plant breeder is the fact that many of his early varieties are still popular today, botanically identified as *Nymphaea × marliacea*, the "×" signifying the plants' hybrid origins. When Marliac was invited by the Royal Horticultural Society to deliver a lecture about his water lilies, he declared that their exquisite color range was the result of using pollen from multicolored tropical water lilies. The audience swallowed his story, for several nurserymen rushed off to collect tropical pollen to imitate his methods. Unfortunately, nothing fruitful ever came from these endeavors, for today we know that hardy water lilies and tropicals are incompatible for crossbreeding, and there is no tropical parentage in any of Marliac's varieties. Marliac deliberately deceived his audience because he did not wish to reveal his secrets!

By the time Monet painted **Water Lilies (1906),** he had begun to depict his water garden at close range, concentrating on the exquisite water lilies and their reflections mirrored in the still water. The absence of a horizon line also characterizes much of his later work; this technique creates a sense of mystery in the composition. The soft pinks and quiet greens coupled with the hazy blue of the reflected sky promote a sense of tranquility, a hallmark of Monet's water garden. He saved riotous color and lively plant combinations for his flower garden, the Clos Normand.

Chapter Five

THE CLOS NORMAND

"Monet is, perhaps, seen at his best, and certainly in his most genial mood, when, cigar for company, he strolls around his propriete at Giverny, discussing the mysteries of propagation, grafts and color schemes, with his small army of blue-bloused, sabotted gardeners."

—WYNFORD DEWHURST, BRITISH JOURNALIST, DESCRIBING A VISIT TO MONET'S GARDEN

Billowing tree-form roses are an elegant feature of Monet's flower garden. The cascading effect is achieved by a wire umbrella frame held high to support the topknot of roses.

THE TERM *CLOS NORMAND* REFERS TO A NORMAN GARDEN, ALTHOUGH THE USUAL WORD FOR GARDEN IS JARDIN. FOR THE FRENCH, A CLOS NORMAND CONJURES UP A PARTICULAR TYPE OF GARDEN—AN INTIMATE COUNTRY GARDEN, VERY INFORMAL AND FLOWERY, SIMILAR IN STYLE TO AN ENGLISH COTTAGE GARDEN. AT THE TURN OF THE CENTURY, NORMANDY STILL HAD MANY QUAINT COTTAGES WITH THATCHED ROOFS, HARDLY DISTINGUISHABLE FROM THATCHED COTTAGES IN ENGLAND, WITH THEIR TINY FLOWER GARDENS BRIGHT WITH COLOR.

COTTAGE GARDENS

Shortly after serving in the French military in North Africa, Monet felt it necessary to leave France during a period of civil unrest. For almost nine months, from the summer of 1870 to the autumn of 1871, he stayed in England, painting as much

The name of Monet's flower garden, Le Clos Normand, suggests an intimate flower-filled sanctuary.

as he could and studying the works of English landscape painters such as Constable and Turner. One of his best friends in France, the Impressionist painter Albert Sisley, was an Englishman who helped Monet make some good contacts and explore the English countryside.

Gardening in Britain was undergoing a revolution. Influential gardeners such as Gertrude Jekyll and William Robinson were extolling the benefits of informality, pleading for an end to formal, Victorian-style carpet bedding schemes in favor of mixed borders and woodland and meadow gardens, with an eye toward pleasing color combinations and foliage contrasts with panache.

Monet liked this new English style of gardening, and his property at Giverny later afforded him the space to translate the English style to his own taste. He even subscribed to a beautiful new British magazine, *Country Life*, which carried a regular gardening column by Gertrude Jekyll, herself a great admirer of Impressionist art. Her writings undoubtedly fell on fertile ground and gave Monet food for thought, but an even greater influence on the gardening philosophy Monet applied to the Clos Normand was his friend Gustave Caillebotte.

THE INFLUENCE
OF CAILLEBOTTE'S GARDEN

Caillebotte was a marine engineer who was born to a wealthy family with a 24-acre (10-hectare) estate at Yerres. He learned a great deal about gardening from a staff of professional gardeners who tended the family's parklike estate and expansive vegetable garden. Caillebotte was a great inspiration to all the Impressionist painters. He not only sponsored their exhibitions, he also bought their work to keep them fed and supplied with art materials. And he shared with them his love of gardening.

When the Caillebotte family estate was sold, Caillebotte purchased a property of his own at Petit Gennevilliers, west of Paris, and established a garden there several years before Monet moved to Giverny. The property had a pink house and a long, narrow acre of ground in the back. Caillebotte's property fronted the Seine, where he maintained a boat dock and a mooring for a sailboat. These elements were all ones Monet found exceedingly attractive, and which he borrowed freely when he began to garden at Giverny.

THE IMPORTANCE OF PERSPECTIVE

Caillebotte was a skillful Impressionist artist in his own right, and he painted water reflections thirty years before Monet attempted them. Caillebotte's specialty was painting scenes with powerful lines of perspective, and his style influenced Monet to establish a flower garden like his own, with similar strong lines. It didn't matter that both Caillebotte's and Monet's exuberant plantings would soon obscure the geometric beds; the most

PERFECT PARTNERS

YELLOW 'CONNECTICUT KING' AND ORANGE 'ENCHANTMENT' ASIATIC LILIES COMBINE WITH YELLOW LOOSESTRIFE (*LYSIMACHIA PUNCTATA*) TO CREATE A HOT COLOR HARMONY ALONG THE BOTTOM OF THE CLOS NORMAND IN EARLY SUMMER. THE METAL RAILING IN THE BACKGROUND USED TO BE OPEN SO PASSERSBY COULD PEER OVER THE WALL, BUT NOW A DENSE FIRETHORN HEDGE, INSTALLED FOR SECURITY REASONS, OBSCURES THE VIEW.

important design concepts were long swathes of color and infinite depth, created by long beds and borders. When viewed from above, these corridors of color could be painted as narrow floral avenues or, when viewed from across, as waves of color.

Caillebotte's own garden no longer survives; it was obliterated to make room for industrial development. But it is possible to reconstruct the formal design by studying Caillebotte's paintings and photographs of his garden. Although smaller in size than Monet's garden, the similarity is quite obvious.

Unfortunately, Caillebotte died in middle age from a brain tumor, and Monet lost not only one of his best friends and patrons, but also his gardening mentor.

Above: *Rectangular beds of color called* **plante bands** *create strong lines of perspective looking up from the bottom of the Clos Normand. The plantings here show a hot color harmony derived mainly from Siberian and English wallflowers in beds edged with lilac-blue aubretia.*

Opposite: *At first glance,* **Monet's Garden at Giverny (1900)** *seems to show diagonal beds of a single hue of irises bordering the Grande Allée. Closer inspection reveals that there are actually several shades of blue and lavender irises, some of which feature white upper petals, a combination that produces a bright, glittering effect.*

CLEARING THE SITE

We know that when Monet first moved to the Pink House, the landscape featured an orchard with dreary lines of boxwood and some large spruce. Little by little he cleared the orchard, delegating the boxwood to his brush pile. He wanted to remove the too-tall spruce, but his wife could not bear the thought of seeing such old trees destroyed. So a compromise was reached; he decapitated them. This clearing of the site produced a 2½-acre (1-hectare) sunny space in which he decided to grow mostly flowers. Beds were dug and amended with stable manure and peat. At first he was aided in his endeavors only by his family: his wife, two sons, stepson, and five stepdaughters. About the time that Monet moved to Giverny, when he was forty-six, his fortunes began to improve. Exhibitions in the United States brought him some substantial sales from paintings, and soon he was able to hire a team of gardeners. But Monet always ruled the garden with an iron will. Whenever he had to leave on a trip he left detailed notes about when to start seeds, buy bulbs, strike cuttings, move plants out of cold frames, and prune his roses. He was impatient of error, flying into a rage if his instructions were not carried out to the letter. Once when he failed to get approval from the local authorities to enlarge his water lily garden, he cursed the mayor (saying "shit on his head!"), and told the gardeners to throw all the plants he had bought into the river. They didn't, and with a little more persistence Monet was able to get the necessary permits.

PATCHWORK EFFECTS

Monet laid out his Clos Normand flower garden around its central axis, the Grande Allée. To the west he had fifteen narrow rectangular borders running the length of his garden, which he used to display bearded irises. To the east he had thirty-eight smaller "paintbox" beds that look like cemetery plots in the winter. Today these beds are intensively planted to create color harmonies throughout the growing season. No bed is allowed to fade until closing day on October 31. This was not

Opposite: *The formal layout of the Clos Normand is evident in this high elevation view, looking from the bottom of the garden toward the house in early spring. As tulips and wallflowers fade, irises, peonies, and poppies begin to bloom.*

PERFECT PARTNERS

ACROSS ONE OF MONET'S LAWNS, LILAC-PINK AUTUMN CROCUS (*COLCHICUM AUTUMNALE*) HAVE BEEN PLANTED IN DRIFTS. TO ACHIEVE THE CHARMING EFFECT OF FLOWERING BULBS CONTRASTING WITH MANICURED GRASS, PEEL BACK THE TURF AND LOOSEN AND CONDITION THE SOIL BENEATH TO CREATE A SPECIAL PLANTING BED. PLANT THE BULBS IN THE CONDITIONED SOIL AND THEN ROLL THE TURF BACK INTO PLACE. IN AUTUMN YOUR LAWN WILL BE DOTTED WITH THESE TINY TREASURES.

so in Monet's time. He generally massed a particular variety of flowering annual or biennial in each bed, rather like the trial gardens of English and French seed houses, so that the whole presented a patchwork quilt effect. Most of these beds reached their flowering peak in early summer with an abundance of annuals, such as larkspur, snapdragons, and China asters.

You can create your own patchwork plantings on a smaller scale by dividing your beds into small, regular spaces. By choosing long-flowering annuals like *Salvia farinacea* 'Victoria', *Salvia coccinea* 'Lady in Red', spider flowers (*Cleome hasslerana*), and 'Fantasia' impatiens, you can keep your beds beautiful all summer long. To extend the season of bloom into autumn, try planting cushion chrysanthemums and dwarf perennial asters in among the summer annuals, and use solid blocks of a particular color rather than mixtures.

Tiers of color face each other across the Grande Allée, with nasturtiums forming the bottom tier, New England asters the middle, and sunflowers the top tier.

TIERS OF COLOR

In composing his planting schemes in the Clos Normand, Monet liked to have at least three levels of color interest: low-growing plants that served as an edging and provided interest up to waist height; some plants for eye-level interest; and finally some tall elements, particularly plants that complemented the blue sky. For example, a common planting scheme along the Grande Allée for the autumn is orange nasturtiums and red dahlias for ground-level interest, mauve New England asters for eye-level color, and tall yellow perennial sunflowers as towering accents. The result is color that extends to every level, even when the climbing roses that are a main feature of the Grande Allée in summer are finished blooming.

CONTRASTS OF LIGHT AND SHADE

An important visual effect for Monet was pronounced contrasts of light and shade, particularly from the dark, silhouetted forms of foreground features such as spiky plants. Shadow patterns, framed views, and leaf tunnels also created the satisfying contrasts of light and shade Monet admired.

To create contrasts of light in a small garden devoid of tall, billowing trees, consider bringing in some mature trees in Versailles-style planters, or create a vine-covered arbor. The dappled shade thrown by deciduous trees or tall, vine-covered accents brings a unique illusion of texture to your garden, offering interesting contrasts as shards of light play across your underplantings.

The branches of a mature spruce tree frame the Clos Normand. Note how the shadowy tones and spiky flowers in the foreground create a beautiful dark contrast to the rest of the garden, which is flooded in sunlight. Monet deliberately designed his garden so that he could paint contrasts of light and shade, as well as shadow patterns.

MONET'S BEARDED IRISES

Of all the plants in the Clos Normand, two plant families meant more to Monet than all others—his roses and his bearded irises (*Iris × germanica*). Monet loved the bearded iris for its infinite color range. Although shades of blue are most often associated with bearded irises, they come in every color of the rainbow, including red, yellow, green, ginger, black, and white. Indeed, the bearded iris family has so many shades that some defy color classification. Many of them are also bicolored or tricolored, changing hue according to the intensity of light. Most bearded irises bloom in late May and early June, with many other substantial hardy perennials such as herbaceous peonies and Oriental poppies. When these three chieftains of the perennial race bloomed together in the Clos Normand, Monet considered the garden to be at its zenith.

PERFECT PARTNERS

THE DEEP BLUE BEARDED IRISES 'LILAC HAZE' AND 'BLUE REFLECTION' ARE PERFECT COMPLEMENTS TO YELLOW SIBERIAN WALLFLOWERS. BLUE AND YELLOW IS AN EVER-POPULAR COLOR COMBINATION FOR THE GARDEN, AND THESE FLOWERS BRING OFF THE SCHEME IN STUNNING FASHION.

PERFECT PARTNERS

BEARDED IRISES IN PALE LAVENDER AND 'WEDGWOOD' BLUE DUTCH IRISES, PAIRED WITH PINK COTTAGE TULIPS, PRODUCE A RESTFUL BLUE AND PINK COLOR HARMONY. NOTE THAT FOR BEARDED IRISES AND TULIPS TO BLOOM TOGETHER IT'S ESSENTIAL TO CHOOSE AN EARLY-FLOWERING BEARDED IRIS CULTIVAR AND A LATE-FLOWERING TULIP CULTIVAR.

MONET'S ROSES

A s the irises fade from view, the roses start to dominate the Clos Normand. They are planted in every conceivable manner—as flowering shrubs, as climbers, even trained to a single trunk to form a standard, or tree-shaped rose. Moreover, Monet's collection included both old garden roses and the more modern, large-flowered hybrid teas. Among the first to bloom, in late spring, is 'Mermaid', a thorny, yellow, single-flowered climber with a large saucer shape. It also has distinctive foliage, which is almost bright red in its juvenile form, and later turns a rich, lustrous dark green.

'Mermaid' was introduced in 1918 by English rosarian William Paul, who also was responsible for introducing another Monet favorite, 'Paul's Scarlet' two years earlier. 'Paul's Scarlet' is an incredibly floriferous, scarlet-red rose with vigorous canes. In June the blooms are often so dense that they almost completely hide the foliage.

Another important rose development in Monet's time was 'La Belle Vichyssoise'. This shrub displayed curtains of deep pink but-

Top: *A pink-flowering shrub rose has been grafted onto a tall straight rose trunk to create an avalanche of blossoms that echo the pink stucco of the main house.* **Above:** *'Paul's Scarlet' climbing rose covers a metal trellis, framing pale flowers that create an illusion of distance. Background plants include white dame's rocket and pink campion.*

tonlike roses, held in clusters on strong canes that could reach 30 feet (9 meters) high. During this period—1820 to 1920—so many new plant species and hybrids were introduced (more than at any other time in horticultural history) that it is known today as the Golden Age of Horticulture. Certainly no one took greater advantage of this floral extravaganza than Monet. Today 'La Belle Vichyssoise' is difficult to find, but a good substitute is 'American Pillar', which Monet undoubtedly acquired from the Conard Pyle Company, in West Grove, Pennsylvania.

A particularly clear visual impression of Monet's roses and his passion for collecting both old and new varieties was penned by Monet's friend Gustave Geffroy: "It is the moment of the roses, all the marvels with glorious names surround you with their variations and fragrances. They are planted at intervals on bushes, on hedges, on trellises, climbing walls, clinging to pillars and arches on the central pathway. There are the most unusual and the most ordinary, which are not the least beautiful, the simple roses, the clusters of sweetbriar, the brightest and the palest."

Gladioli (1876) shows a hot color harmony that features gladiolus and a richly patterned background of diagonal trelliswork. Most important, though, is Monet's clever use of black violas, like pinpricks of paint, among geraniums, to create a shimmering sensation. Butterflies heighten the sensation of a garden flooded with light.

BUTTERFLIES

Monet did not need to grow special plants to attract butterflies because he grew so many brightly colored annuals, which naturally attract butterflies. He obviously loved the presence of butterflies, for they not only introduced flickering movement to the garden, they added a sense of shimmer. This is especially evident in his marvelous painting entitled *Gladioli* (1876), in which a flock of butterflies dances above a bed of spiky red and pink gladiolus and red geraniums. A woman with a parasol stands serene and silent, as if trying not to disturb the flights of butterflies. The flower bed also features what appear to be black violas in company with silvery blue flowers, creating a distinct shimmering sensation. Some dark elements in the background, such as trelliswork and a stockade fence, heighten the effect of sunlight streaming onto the flower bed.

The butterfly bush (*Buddleia davidii*) attracts butterflies like honey draws bees. Planting a variety of bright-colored annuals will entice butterflies to your garden as well. They are particularly fond of orange and red flowers with trumpet-shaped blooms. Open sunny spaces planted with lots of nectar-producing flowers and sources of food for the larvae will ensure that these winged visitors are drawn irresistibly to your garden.

ANNUALS, PERENNIALS, AND FLOWERING BULBS

Color in the Clos Normand is maintained by a parade of annuals, perennials, and flowering bulbs, which combine with the roses in a showy display. Monet's favorite perennials include clematis, lavender, hollyhocks, gladiolus, dahlias, and verbascums. Summer-blooming annuals include pastel China asters, red geraniums, blood red love-lies-bleeding, pale pink cosmos, white nicotiana, and pink spider flowers. Many flowering bulbs, such as daffodils and tulips, are important components of the spring flowering display, while in summer and autumn the vibrant colors of tuberous

dahlias and gladiolus combine with New England asters, chrysanthemums, and perennial sunflowers to finish the season.

Again, we have Gustave Geffroy to thank for a vivid description of annuals and perennials mingling their charms: "Each month is adorned with its flowers, from the lilacs and irises to the chrysanthemums and nasturtiums. The azaleas, the hydrangeas, the foxgloves, the hollyhocks, the forget-me-nots, the violets—the sumptuous flowers and the modest ones mingle and follow one another on this ever-ready soil, wonderfully tended by the experienced gardeners under the infallible eye of the master."

The garden was put to bed with the killing frosts of autumn, and Monet would spend much of the winter studying garden magazines, garden books, and mail-order catalogs. The garden would come alive again in April, with the flowering of thousands of daffodils beneath ornamental cherries and crab apples.

The plante bands, *when viewed across, become waves of color. Here, perennial sunflowers, dahlias, and impatiens (foreground) are framed by the shadowy branches of a spruce, creating a "window" along the Grande Allée.*

THE VEGETABLE GARDEN

"Florimond knew Monet's rages if the

vegetables were not picked at the right time, yet

nothing was more difficult."

—CLAIRE JOYES, *MONET'S TABLE*

Cordoned apple trees border a lawn in Monet's Clos Normand. Fruit trees won space in his flower garden because of their decorative spring blossoms, but Monet did not generally like to mix plantings of flowers and vegetables, which he grew at the Blue House on a separate property.

A GARDENER KNOWN ONLY AS FLORIMOND SUPERVISED MONET'S VEGETABLE GARDEN. WHENEVER HE NEEDED EXTRA HELP, SUCH AS DURING THE SPRING PLANTING, HE BORROWED GARDENERS FROM MONET'S FLOWER GARDENS. MONET NOT ONLY SUPERVISED THE SELECTION OF VEGETABLES FOR EACH DAY'S MEAL, HE TOOK SPECIAL CARE TO CHOOSE THOSE REQUIRED FOR THE STOCKPOT, TO MAKE THE STEWS AND BROTHS THE FAMILY ENJOYED DURING THE WEEK. ❧ THE HOUSEHOLD WAS RUN ON A STRICT SCHEDULE, DEVISED TO GIVE MONET THE MAXIMUM AMOUNT OF TIME TO PAINT. SINCE HE FAVORED MORNING LIGHT ABOVE ALL ELSE, HE WOULD RISE AT THE BREAK OF DAWN AND EAT A HEARTY BREAKFAST BEFORE SALLYING FORTH INTO HIS GARDEN OR INTO THE COUNTRYSIDE IN SEARCH OF A MOTIF. LUNCH WAS SERVED AT ELEVEN THIRTY, TO GIVE HIM TIME TO PREPARE FOR PAINTING IN AFTERNOON LIGHT. LUNCH WAS THE ONLY TIME OF DAY MONET WOULD ENTERTAIN VISITORS, AND HE WOULD BECOME IRRITABLE IF ANYONE DAWDLED OVER THEIR MEAL. IF A VISITOR WAS A SLOW EATER HE WAS NEVER OFFERED SECONDS. MONET USUALLY ATE DINNER ALONE WITH HIS FAMILY PROMPTLY AT SEVEN O'CLOCK, AND HE INVARIABLY WENT TO BED BY NINE THIRTY.

Monet's kitchen and dining room are themselves works of art. The kitchen is covered in Delft blue tiles from Holland, and sports beautiful shining copperware and an immense black stove, all of which combined to creat a bold color composition. Cooking there with bright light flooding through lace-curtained windows was obviously a great pleasure, and though Monet maintained a cook and a butler, the kitchen too seems to have been the master's domain.

The dining room is spacious, decorated in a cheerful blue and yellow color combination. Monet even had a blue and yellow table service to match the decor. The table centerpiece was always a carefully chosen composition of flowers fresh from the garden. Whether Monet was painting *en plein air*, ensconced in his studio, puttering in the garden, or enjoying a fabulous meal, his world was filled with color and light. He is well deserving of his reputation as the world's first colorist.

The house Monet lived in at Giverny has pink stucco walls and green shutters. At one time it was called the Cider Press, but after Monet spruced it up it was affectionately dubbed the Pink House. The house where Monet maintained his vegetable garden

became known as the Blue House. To distinguish between the two properties, he had the walls of the second house painted bright blue—the very same color as a house he had admired and painted in Holland (*Blue House at Zaanden*, 1871). It is possible that Monet's painting *The Roses* (1915) was done at the Blue House, for it depicts a bush of pink roses arching its flowering canes against a sheet of blue in the same tone as the facade of the Blue House. A bush of pale pink roses still flowers each spring along the driveway in front of the Blue House.

FLOWER-BORDERED VEGETABLE PLOTS

Monet's vegetable garden, which he referred to as his "formal garden," was a 2½-acre (1-hectare) plot divided into large geometric beds to accommodate different families of vegetables. A marvelous painting of Monet's vegetable garden by American Impressionist painter Willard Metcalf has recently come to light. It shows large rectangular beds of lettuce and cabbage laid out like quilt blocks and completely surrounded by

Monet's Formal Garden (1885), *by American Impressionist painter Willard Metcalf, is the only known painting showing Monet's vegetable garden. The painting shows geometrically shaped vegetable plots outlined by hedges of herbaceous peonies. Surrounding the entire garden is a high wall covered with espaliered fruit trees.*

hedges of herbaceous peonies. Moreover, one can clearly see that the surrounding wall was covered in espaliered fruit trees, including apples, pears, peaches, apricots, figs, grapes, and plums.

Metcalf was the first American painter to visit Monet. He is reported to have called upon Monet with two friends in 1885, and could hardly believe his luck when they were invited to lunch. After the meal, Metcalf requested permission to paint Monet's flower garden, but Monet suggested that the vegetable garden would make a better subject. Monet's stepdaughter Blanche Hoschedé accompanied Metcalf to the vegetable garden, where he was allowed to paint. The resulting work—in oil on canvas—is a beautiful overall view of the geometrically shaped plots of leafy vegetables bordered by red, pink, and white peonies in full bloom.

A Small-Space Monet-Style Vegetable Garden

You don't need a 2½-acre (1-hectare) site to create the same effect that Monet achieved in his vegetable garden. This scaled-down version is only 32 by 36 feet (10 by 11m), and a modified version can be executed in a space as small as 8 by 10 feet (2.5 by 3m). The rectangular vegetable beds, coupled with the garden's flower border, are reminiscent of an old-fashioned quilt design.

No matter what size garden you are planning, there are several essential elements required in a Monet-style vegetable garden. First, the garden must be divided into four planting spaces, a design that imparts a formal air and serves a practical purpose as well. The four areas can be used to rotate crops from one year to the next; moving crops from one quadrant to another in successive years reduces the risk of disease. You may use frilly red and green leaf lettuce to create the quilt pattern, or you may choose a variety of spring-maturing leafy vegetables, such as cabbage, spinach, scallions, and endive in combination with each other or with lettuce.

Another important element to the vegetable garden is the hedge of flowers that completely surrounds the site. Monet planted double hedges, but a single row will suffice in this smaller space. Peonies in a delicate mix of red, pink, and white are traditional for the border planting, but any early-flowering plants can be substituted to achieve the desired contrast of flowers with the lush foliage of the planted quadrants. Particularly successful as hedges are annual flowers with red, pink, and white in their color range—consider English daisies, pansies, cinerarias, geraniums, or snapdragons.

Finally, a fence of cordoned fruit trees separates the vegetable plots from the flower hedge. (See "Espaliered Fruit Trees" on page 99). Monet used apple and pear trees, but you may choose to substitute peach, nectarine, plum, or apricot trees, or grow a combination of fruit trees.

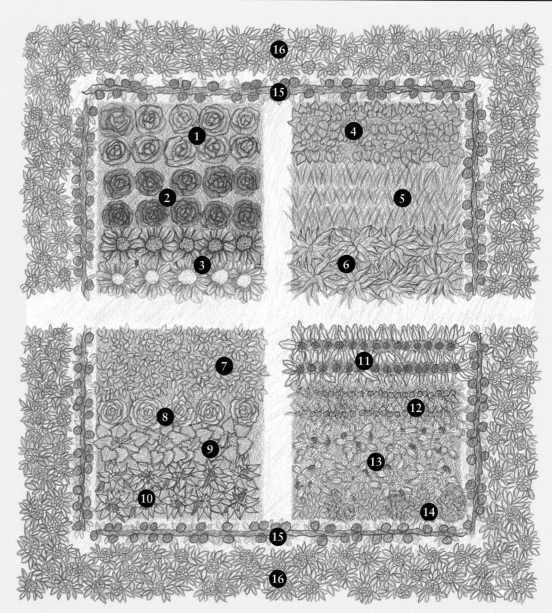

PLANT LIST

1. Green cabbage
2. Red cabbage
3. Broccoli/cauliflower
4. Bush beans
5. Onions
6. Sweet corn
7. English peas followed by zucchini
8. Lettuce followed by chard
9. Summer squash
10. Peppers
11. Beets
12. Carrots
13. Tomatoes
14. Parsley and basil
15. Cordoned apple fence
16. Peony hedge

ESPALIERED FRUIT TREES

Monet mixed flowers and vegetables only in his vegetable garden, though his Clos Normand flower garden does feature some espaliered apple and pear trees, as well as some cordon-trained fruit trees as an edging around lawn areas. Every inch of wall space around the vegetable garden appears to have been covered with espaliered fruit trees. The style of design is indistinct, but it is likely that Monet copied Caillebotte's espaliered fruit tree designs, which included training patterns known as fan, diamond, upright, and horizontal.

In addition to growing espalier forms against walls, Monet trained his fruit trees to form freestanding fences. His favorite design, called a "double cordon" (*cordon* meaning rope), was used to create low, living fences for edging lawns or flower beds.

Growing trees in espalier forms or as cordons is an art challenging to even the most experienced gardener. It requires coaxing the branches into a single plane and constantly pinching back unwanted shoots while training other branches into the desired form. If you want to try your hand at Monet's double cordon design, plant a line of fruit trees at equal distances (4 feet [1.2 meters] is the preferred distance). Train one tree so that its branches are splayed into a T-shape at a height of about 3 feet (1 meter), to form the upper tier, or "fence rail." The next tree in the row is then trained so that its branches form a T at a level of about 1½ feet (0.5 meters), to form the lower tier or fence rail.

Left: *Cordoned apple trees offer blush-tinted blossoms in spring. Monet used these natural fences to encircle flower beds and areas of lawn.* **Above:** *In autumn the cordoned trees bear plump, crisp, juicy apples. Trees trained in this manner often produce heavy yields, as they get excellent air circulation and can be judiciously pruned.*

COLORFUL VEGETABLES

Monet liked to experiment with anything unusual and edible. Mushrooms were grown in the basement of the Blue House, and for a while Monet apparently had a liking for Chinese artichokes, a tuberous pink relative of the Jerusalem artichoke. The color of vegetables and fruits was obviously as important to Monet as the color of flowers, since he occasionally rendered them in still lifes when the weather was too bad for him to venture outside. A particularly beautiful arrangement, *Still Life with Melon* (1876), shows an orange-fleshed melon with an unusual warty skin sliced open at the ribs to form a luscious crown, with a mound of reddish-maroon peaches piled high in a dish against a Chinese willow-pattern plate. The colors are so bright and appetizing the fruits seem to glow with freshness.

Since Monet's day tremendous strides have been made in breeding new varieties of vegetables. Monet would no doubt be overjoyed to discover that, in addition to red and green, there are now orange, yellow, chocolate-colored, and black sweet bell peppers. There is even a variety called 'Rainbow' (also known as 'Islander'), which has black, lavender, yellow, orange, and red fruits all on the same plant! The shapes and colors of hot peppers are even more extensive.

Similarly, there is a marvelous new multicolored Swiss chard called 'Rainbow'. In Monet's day Swiss chard was available only with white stalks, but now there are stalks of yellow, orange, apricot, pink, crimson, and cream. Chard is so closely related to beets that they are able to cross-pollinate, and so even beets have undergone a colorful revolution—in addition to the familiar dark red, there is a scarlet-red called 'Chiogga' and a golden variety known as 'Burpee's Golden'. Put these beets together in a harvest

One of Monet's favorite vegetables was red cabbage, which he ate cooked and pickled. His paintings suggest that he liked fruits and vegetables with strong colors as much for their visual appeal as for their flavor.

arrangement with orange carrots and purple-top turnips for a spectacular multicolored assortment of root crops as appealing as any pepper arrangement!

Among today's tomatoes, there are not only red varieties, but yellow, orange, maroon, pink, green, and white. Even eggplants—aubergines to Monet—come not only in the familiar black and purple-skinned varieties, but in white and striped varieties. New varieties of pumpkins and squash are even more alluring—'Lakota' is a large, pear-shaped variety with a beautiful red and dark green marbled skin; 'Carnival' is an acorn squash with green and yellow mottled skin; and 'Delicata' has creamy, torpedo-shaped fruits with handsome green stripes and a rich orange flesh. The flavor of these winter squashes, similar to the taste of sweet potatoes, is simply wonderful.

COLD FRAMES

There were cold frames in the vegetable garden, which served for frost protection. This enabled the Monet household to remain largely self-sufficient for six months of the year. In addition to the prodigious quantities of fruits and vegetables he grew, Monet also maintained pens at the Pink House for raising chickens, ducks, turkeys, and rabbits.

Filled with brilliant colors and textures, and overflowing with fresh and healthful vegetables, Monet's vegetable garden was a source of pleasure visually and yielded much of the family's daily fare. Plant your own formal vegetable garden in Monet's distinctive style for a backyard that is both beautiful and productive.

Above Left: While this 'Rainbow' Swiss chard, with its gold, crimson, and white stalks, is a modern plant-breeding achievement, the dramatic colors would have appealed to Monet. Above Right: This cold frame is a surviving relic of Caillebotte's vegetable garden, and here holds lettuce and zucchini. Cold frames like this were used by Monet to grow early vegetable crops.

Chapter Seven

TREES, SHRUBS, AND VINES

*"I would love to do orange and lemon trees
silhouetted against the blue sky, but I cannot
find them the way I want them....it's all...
a confused mass of foliage which is terribly
difficult to render. I'm really the man for
isolated trees and broad spaces."*

—MONET, WRITING HOME FROM
A TOUR OF THE MEDITERRANEAN

Bordering Monet's pond, fragrant 'Exbury' hybrid azaleas present a
dramatic sunset-colored harmony against a backdrop of strong skyline
trees, including weeping willow and purple beech.

TREES AND OTHER WOODY PLANTS WERE A FAVORITE MOTIF OF MONET'S, AND THEY WERE ESSENTIAL TO THE SUCCESS OF HIS GARDEN. GEORGES TRUFFAUT NOTED SOME OF THE BEST PLANTS IN THE FOLLOWING DESCRIPTION OF A WALK THROUGH THE WATER GARDEN: "ON ONE SHORE, FORMING A BACKDROP, THERE IS A CLUSTER OF BRIAR PLANTS AMONG WHICH FERNS, KALMIA, RHODODENDRONS, AND HOLLY PREDOMINATE. SHADE ALONG THE WATER'S EDGE IS PROVIDED BY HARDY TREE ROSES, OR ROSES CLIMBING ALONG EXISTING TREES. IN ORDER TO ACHIEVE THIS HE MADE SPECIAL USE OF AN EXTRAORDINARY HARDY ROSE CALLED 'LA BELLE VICHYSSOISE', WHICH GROWS 21 TO 24 FEET [6.4 TO 7.2M] HIGH AND PRODUCES LONG CLUSTERS OF SMALL SCENTED BLOOMS."

Truffaut also mentions being impressed by Monet's large grove of bamboo, which grew up to 24 feet (7.2 meters) high, and the vanhouttei spiraea mixing its snow white blossoms with the feathery, powder pink blooms of tamarix.

Monet's trees, shrubs, and vines, like the rest of his garden, were intended to be painted, and his own very personal artistic style dictated his planting choices. An influence on Monet's work as artist and gardener that is often overlooked by both art historians and horticulturists is Monet's early success as a caricaturist. Even in his teens Monet made money selling cartoons in the channel port of Le Havre, where his parents had moved from Paris to run a wholesale food supply business that provisioned ships.

At first, Monet seems to have tried hard to abandon his cartoon style, but his early oil paintings are unremarkable, consisting of clichéd compositions of churches and fishermen's cottages in somber tones. Monet's style came alive when his compositions became more animated in line and color, exaggerated by the dynamics of light and atmosphere.

Monet obviously felt that his background as a cartoonist was important to his education and success as an artist. In an interview with journalist André Arnyvelde he spoke enthusiastically about his early years, saying, "Even as a small child I was good at caricatures. I drew them on my notebooks in class... I amused myself drawing caricatures. Everywhere and anywhere: at the theater, in cafes, at the homes I visited. At first I just gave the drawings to the people they represented. Then when they began to argue over them, well my word! I started charging for them!

"One day a gentleman comes up to me in the framer's shop and says 'Your drawings are interesting; they show clear strengths. You should try something beside caricatures. Come see me, and I'll give you a few pointers.'" It was Eugène Boudin, a painter who spent almost all of his life on the Normandy coast capturing seascapes. Monet accompanied Boudin on some of his painting excursions and learned about the transience of light, the importance of atmosphere, and above all the strength of painting on the spot, rather than in a studio.

Monet's collection of Japanese woodblock prints also gives a clue to his preference for an animated style of artistic expression. A pair of Japanese cranes striking humorous unbirdlike poses and a busy bee pollinating chrysanthemum flowers are examples of simple but striking compositions in his Japanese print collection; they are almost caricatures in the style of their simplistic composition.

When Monet combines his outlook as a cartoonist, and its exaggeration of line and color, with his skills as a painter of atmosphere and light, we see some of his finest work. Examples include the poplar tree series, with the trees' truncated forms creating stark patterns against an autumn sky; his views of the Seine shrouded in mist, the billowing, cloudlike forms of trees

Haystacks near Giverny (1891) *is one of a series of paintings that dramatizes not only the sinuous trunks of poplar trees, but their decorative bark and animated presence in the landscape.*

appearing ghostlike on the banks; and his *Magpie* (1868) with the mischievous bird sitting audaciously on a wattle fence in a snow-covered garden. Even his *Impression, Sunrise* (1872), which gave Impressionism its name, is an animated view of the misty harbor at Le Havre, with a bright orange sun burning through the haze, and the waves seeming to catch fire from shafts of intense, orange, reflected light.

Later, when Monet began gardening, his Impressionist's eye discovered the potential for dramatic planting schemes such as big, cheerful, yellow sunflowers that contrasted with the blue Seine; tousled clumps of irises spilling onto a gravel pathway with sinuous tree trunks supporting a canopy of freshly unfurled foliage; and larger-than-life arches supporting an avalanche of red blossoms among rich green leaves. Monet's obvious delight in the animated earned scorn from one art critic, who said that Monet's painting of Antibes on the shores of the Mediterranean, framed by the arching branches of what appears to be an olive tree, was flawed because he felt the tree had too many branches and too much foliage to be supported by the slender trunk!

SKYLINE EFFECTS

Monet recognized early in his painting career that trees are the dominant life forms of a landscape. Few natural landscape features add character and a sense of place to an area more than trees, whether they are planted in a grove or as specimens to provide a dramatic accent. Trees produce wonderful shapes against the skyline, especially when silhouetted by a sunset. Even a bare tracery of branches can identify a pine, a beech, or a poplar tree. Each of these types of tree is distinctive in its habit of growth, and the shores of Monet's water garden feature all of them. In the water garden, trees are important not only as skyline decorations, but for the water reflections they create. Monet's choice of woody plants (such as wisteria, bamboo, and willows) for his water garden is especially effective in creating a distinct Japanese sensibility that sets it apart from other gardens.

There are many reports of the extraordinary measures Monet would take to preserve the dra-

Beautiful skyline effects, created by a panorama of different tree shapes and a wealth of foliage colors, are a distinctive feature of Monet's water garden.

matic outlines of trees he was painting, including paying a farmer to delay the felling of certain poplar trees that were crucial to his famous poplars series. The most remarkable story, however, concerns Monet's painting a stark, dormant deciduous tree growing along a craggy coastal walk one day in early spring. When it started to rain too heavily for him to continue, he retired to a nearby village and patiently waited out a week of inclement weather. After the rain stopped and he ventured onto the clifftop meadow with his paints and easel, he discovered to his dismay that the tree had leafed out, hiding its majestic silhouette. Monet persuaded a group of local villagers to come with ladders and strip off every leaf so he could complete his canvas!

THE INFLUENCE OF CÉZANNE

Monet and Paul Cézanne were good friends, and he acquired several of Cézanne's paintings early in the painter's career, recognizing immediately Cézanne's artistic genius. Cézanne was the master of greens and earth tones, using them in exhilarating landscapes of the countryside. Cézanne's garden is located on a hillside with a view of the cathedral of Aix-en-Provence. The one-acre (0.4 hectare) property features a collection of flowering trees and shrubs (such as chestnuts and redbuds) that form leaf tunnels above rustic paths leading to clearings. Cézanne's garden is rich in leaf contrasts, with massive limestone blocks brought in from local quarries to form pedestals for displaying the potted plants he liked to paint.

LEAF TUNNELS

Today, the tapestry effects created by imaginative tree and shrub plantings come together most successfully in the paths along Monet's water garden. Here you encounter a sensational leaf tunnel, which highlights the colors, textures, and forms of foliage plants. Some of these leafy tunnels follow the path; others open out onto the water, as in Monet's painting *Willows at Giverny* (1918).

A leafy tunnel of bamboo graces Monet's water garden path. Monet loved the juxtaposition of a dark, shadowy foreground framing an oasis of light.

PERFECT PARTNERS

THE YELLOW PENDANT BLOSSOMS OF A LABUR-
NUM COMBINE WITH THE WEEPING BRANCHES OF
A WILLOW TO CREATE A GRACEFUL CANOPY OF
FOLIAGE ALONG THE MAIN PATH IN MONET'S
WATER GARDEN. LABURNUM GROWS WILD IN THE
HILLS AROUND GIVERNY, AND MONET USED IT
EXTENSIVELY. THE SILVERY LEAVES OF A TREE
PEONY ADD A THIRD ELEMENT OF FOLIAGE
INTEREST TO THE PICTURE.

Visitors enter the water garden through a dark subterranean tunnel (to avoid crossing a busy highway), and ascend a flight of steps into a natural tunnel of redbud trees. After crossing the Japanese bridge, the path leads through a tunnel of bamboo.

To create a leaf tunnel in your garden you need only to select trees that are fast-growing and that have a tendency

Opposite: Footpath in the Garden (1902) *shows a view looking along Monet's Grand Allée from the bottom of the garden toward the house. The painting emphasizes the beautiful shadow patterns created by breaks in the overhead foliage canopy.*

to arch up and out, creating a "cathedral" effect with their branches. Redbuds (*Cercis canadensis*) and laburnums (especially *Laburnum × vossii*) are particularly good choices since they also produce decorative flowers that carpet the ground with their spent blossoms. Plant the trees opposite each other so that the branches arch up and meet in the middle of the path. While a tunnel several trees long is most dramatic, you need only a few trees to give your garden a subtle touch of the effect.

Also consider creating a leaf tunnel with fast-growing vines, such as wisteria or trumpet creeper (*Campsis radicans*), using sturdy arches or crossbeams to support the vine canopy.

FRAMING A VIEW

Trees provided a wonderful framing device for Monet's compositions. He liked to portray the contrast of light and shade, and many of his paintings show an oasis of light in a shaded part of his garden. The sensation of walking along a shaded path and suddenly emerging into the glare of golden sunlight was immensely satisfying to Monet. He also loved the light as it reflected off the pink stucco of his house or played on a tapestry of greens from sunlit shrubs and trees. Monet enjoyed seeing the silhouettes of spirelike flowers such as gladiolus and verbascum and sword-shaped leaves like those of irises and daylilies; he planted these in the foreground of his gardens, allowing the sunlight to outline their strong shapes.

SINUOUS LINES

It wasn't enough for Monet simply to have a haphazard collection of plants in his garden at Giverny. Every tree and flower served a specific purpose, whether to be painted or simply enjoyed during frequent walks around the garden. Monet seemed to want to prove that shortsighted art critic wrong about his Antibes painting, by making slender vines and slim trunks appear overburdened with branches and foliage. He also went all-out for arboreal structure, from the cloudlike forms of weeping willows on the one hand, to the coiling snakelike trunks of wisteria and contorted trunks of crab apples on the other.

The ability of a tree to display a luxurious canopy usually depends on judicious pruning, and especially on the removal of lower branches to emphasize the canopy. To encourage lush foliage and promote strong, vigorous growth, fertilize your trees regularly, at least once a year, in the autumn. Some trees may also require additional support—if a sinuous limb appears to be too heavy or the trunk has a precarious lean to it, you may need to use a sturdy prop.

Above: *Arches trained with climbing roses frame a vista across Monet's pond, highlighting a planting of azaleas on the far bank.* **Opposite:** *The sinuous lines of a Japanese crab apple, accented by blossoms, etch the sky beside the main house.*

BILLOWING FORMS AND SHIMMERING LEAVES

Monet especially admired the weeping willow, a popular tree in Japanese art, and one that is emblematic of a Japanese-style garden. Local willows flourished along the moist banks of the nearby Seine, and some of Monet's finest tree paintings show them shrouded in mist billowing from both sides of the river.

The willow has leaves with silvery undersides that on a summer's day shimmer when caught by a gust of wind. Most of the Impressionist painters admired the subtle movement of wind blowing through vegetation. Sisley, Renoir, and van Gogh all captured the sensation of movement by painting blustery meadows on a windy day. But none re-created the feeling more successfully than Monet in his painting of poplar trees along the banks of the Epte, near Giverny.

The play of light on the silvery underside of many leaves goes unnoticed by most of us walking in the countryside, and the effect is too difficult for most artists to want to paint, but Monet thrived on challenge, and it was his keen eye and the recognition of unusual motifs that set him apart from other painters of his age. A visitor tramping the fields around Giverny one day was moved to note, "Everything interests him. During a walk we took together, he stopped in front of the most dissimilar motifs, uttering words of admiration, and made me note how noble and how unexpected nature is. The enclosed meadows, smelling of mint, planted with willows and poplars, are as dear to him as the broad horizons."

The billowing form of a pink-flowering crab apple decorates one of Monet's plante bands in the Clos Normand in early spring. The spiky green foliage of bearded irises enters the scene as the crab apple fades.

POLLARDED WILLOWS

In the water garden today willows still grow along the sides of the pond. They stand as accents, unpruned, the weeping branches form curtains that drape from a great height to touch the water. Gaps between these leafy curtains frame elements of the pond, especially water lilies, and this framing effect was a favorite motif for Monet. Along the stream that feeds the pond are pollarded willows (pollarding is a technique that involves cutting the

PERFECT PARTNERS

A POLLARDED WILLOW RADIATES ITS SLEEK
YELLOW JUVENILE BRANCHES AGAINST A BACK-
GROUND OF CHERRY BLOSSOMS IN BUD AND THE
RUGGED BRANCH PATTERN OF AN OAK. MONET
LIKED THE WAY LOCAL FARMERS PRUNED WIL-
LOWS BACK TO THE TRUNK, FORCING SLENDER
NEW BRANCHES CALLED WHIPS, WHICH WERE
USED FOR MAKING WATTLE FENCES AND BASKETS.

branches back to the trunk each winter, forcing new spring growth). The new growth of the willows is bright yellow and does not immediately start to weep, but branches out vertically and horizontally in all directions, creating a beautiful starburst effect. Throughout France and Holland, Monet encountered pollarded willows everywhere in the countryside because farmers needed them to produce "whips" or "withies"—pliable branches that can be used to weave wattle fences and baskets. Monet's pollarded willows create striking silhouettes along streams and hedgerows, and the edge of his stream was a perfect place to display them as a distinctive garden feature.

SHADOW PATTERNS

Monet even took into consideration the shadow patterns that different trees cast. He particularly liked the silk tree (*Albizia julibrissin*) for its delicate, mimosalike foliage, which not only allowed turf grass to grow right up to its trunk but dec-

orated the grass with a delicate tracery of shadows. The texture and colors of bark also came into play in the overall scheme of Monet's garden—the dove gray bark of a beech harmonized with the soothing green daffodil foliage planted among its exposed roots. The whiteness of birches and poplars were also important components of Monet's garden; he used them to reflect the colors of sunsets and sunrises, and to highlight the drifts of blue he loved to plant under trees to brighten shadowy areas.

Planting trees with ornamental bark in your own garden not only recalls the beauty of Monet's designs, it provides you with interesting accents in the garden all through winter. Deciduous trees with delicate, sparse leaves allow a dappling of light, creating interesting shadow patterns on the grass beneath them. In addition to the silk tree Monet favored, try the Empress tree (*Paulownia tomentosa*) for its large, heart-shaped leaves or 'Heritage' river birch (*Betula nigra* 'Heritage') for its fast-growing, tall, pyramidal shape and small, serrated leaves that tremble in the wind.

CARPETING EFFECTS

There is a marvelous moment in May when an ancient wisteria vine along the path encircling Monet's water garden drops its petals and briefly turns the sandy-colored path blue. In other sections of the garden rosy redbuds, yellow laburnum, and pink and red rhododendrons overhang the path with floral canopies that are beautiful in bloom, but even more alluring when the petals drop to the ground and cover the earth like confetti.

Planting shrubs that drop their attractive petals or leaves will contribute this picturesque effect to your own garden. In addition to wisteria, consider planting redbud, laburnum, and rhododendron.

ORCHARDS

Monet found orchards enchanting for their potential to provide an umbrella of blossoms in spring. To enhance the look of the orchard, he planted carpets of wildflowers among the roots of the trees. Monet's groves of trees copied plum and apple orchards in the area—the custom there was to prune away lower limbs, exposing the strong, tall trunks and creating a dense, arching canopy of branches that literally knit together overhead.

It is interesting to note that many other Impressionist painters, including van Gogh, Pissaro, and Gauguin, also saw orchards as alluring motifs. Renoir was so fond of painting a particular vista in his olive orchard that he built a special outdoor studio with glass walls, so he could paint the view repeatedly in all seasons.

You needn't replicate a full orchard to capture the beauty of fruit trees in your backyard. A few apple, pear, or peach trees will often do the trick. Prune them as Monet did for the full effect, and underplant them with wildflowers common to your area. Monet liked oxeye daisies, corn poppies, and wild oat grass.

Above: *This beautiful carpeting effect is produced by sweet woodruff* (Gallium odoratum), *a wild European herb used for flavoring May wine. It has the advantage of tolerating deep shade and flowering with myriad white star-shaped flowers that add a sparkle to the base of a willow tree beside Monet's pond.* **Opposite:** *Pink and white flowering cherry trees provide shade for part of Monet's exedra in early spring. Monet admired the avalanche of blossoms from orchard trees like cherries and apples for the glittering quality they bring to the landscape.*

Chapter Eight

MONET'S PLANT PALETTE

"He had talked to me about his garden . . . told me that he had just received a whole shipment of bulbs, including Japanese lilies, his favorite flower, and that he was expecting any day two or three boxes of seeds——'very expensive'——but which, once they had bloomed, would produce beautiful colors."

—GEORGES CLEMENCEAU, FORMER PREMIER OF FRANCE, REPORTING ON A VISIT TO MONET

Tulips, Dutch irises, bearded irises, and wallflowers combine in a beautiful pink, blue, and yellow color harmony.

THE IMPRESSIONIST PAINTERS WERE KEEN OBSERVERS OF NATURE, AND THEY HAD PARTICULAR REASONS FOR LIKING CERTAIN PLANTS. THE KEY TO MONET'S FONDNESS FOR A PARTICULAR PLANT FAMILY OFTEN LAY IN HIS DISCOVERY OF IT GROWING IN THE FIELDS AROUND HIS HOME. HE ALSO ADMIRED FLOWERS FOR THEIR PETAL COLORS, THEIR HABIT OF GROWTH, THEIR FOLIAGE COLORS, AND THEIR SHAPES. INDEED, HE OFTEN PORTRAYED FLOWERING PLANTS SILHOUETTED AGAINST THE SUN SO THE DETAILS OF THE FLOWERS WERE INDISTINCT BUT THEIR INTERESTING OUTLINE WAS EVIDENT. HE DISLIKED TROPICAL-LOOKING CANNAS, PROBABLY BECAUSE THEIR BANANALIKE LEAVES SEEMED SO OUT OF PLACE IN COTTAGE GARDENS. CANNAS ALSO SHOW A DISPROPORTIONATE AMOUNT OF BARE STEM BEFORE THE GARISH FLOWERS APPEAR. MORE TO HIS LIKING WERE COTTAGE-GARDEN PLANTS SUCH AS DIANTHUS AND DAISIES. ALTHOUGH MONET PAINTED RELATIVELY FEW CLOSE-UPS OF FLOWERS, HE PAINTED MANY SCENES SHOWING THEM IN MASSES. WITH A FEW DEFT BRUSH STROKES IN A STARBURST SHAPE AND A DAB OF YELLOW IN THE MIDDLE, HE COULD QUICKLY REPRESENT THE FORM OF A DAISY. FOLLOWING IS A LIST OF PLANTS MONET GREW IN ABUNDANCE, AND THE REASONS HE LIKED THEM. NOTE THAT THE PHILOSOPHY IN MONET'S GARDEN TODAY IS TO REMAIN FAITHFUL TO THE PAINTER'S DESIGN SENSIBILITIES, PARTICULARLY HIS COLOR HARMONIES, RATHER THAN TO GROW THE IDENTICAL VARIETIES MONET PLANTED. WHERE USEFUL FOR HOME GARDENERS, THE CULTIVARS AND VARIETIES NOW GROWN IN MONET'S GARDEN ARE DETAILED AS WELL.

AGAPANTHUS

Agapanthus (*Agapanthus africanus*) is somewhat tender, and not always capable of surviving outdoors at Giverny. Monet may in fact have overwintered them in his greenhouse. Sometimes called lily-of-the-Nile, agapanthus is most valuable for its sky blue coloring and the large size of its globular flower heads, which consist of tubular flowers in clusters. The flower heads are held aloft on slender stems above foun-

tains of straplike leaves; this is how Monet painted them, with the pond as a background.

Agapanthus are grown from bulbous roots, and they are especially suitable for growing in pots. After flowering outdoors, and at the onset of freezing weather, the pots can be moved inside. The roots will go dormant and survive with little or no water until spring, when they can be revived by watering and exposure to bright light. Flowering occurs during early summer.

BLUE AGAPANTHUS PARTNERED WITH PINK SUM-
MER PHLOX CREATES AN UNUSUAL BUT LOVELY
GARDEN PICTURE. MONET GREATLY ADMIRED THE
LARGE BLUE UMBELS AND TRUMPET-SHAPED
BLOOMS OF AGAPANTHUS. THOUGH AGAPANTHUS
IS NOT RELIABLY HARDY AT GIVERNY, MONET
PROBABLY OVERWINTERED THE PLANTS IN POTS
IN HIS GREENHOUSE.

ASTERS AND CHRYSANTHEMUMS

Monet liked daisies and daisylike plants in his garden. The daisy parade started in early spring with leopard's bane (*Doronicum cordatum*), a shade-loving yellow daisy that grows wild in the woodlands around Giverny; next in line to bloom were oxeye daisies (*Chrysanthemum leucanthemum*) in late spring; then sunflowers (*Helianthus annuus*) in summer; and a flourish in autumn with asters and chrysanthemums. Blue shades of New England and New York hybrid asters are an important component of Monet's Grande Allée in autumn, since they complement the yellow perennial sunflowers and orange nasturtiums, creating a blue-orange-yellow motif.

In *The Garden* (1902), Monet makes parallel beds of asters the focus of a view along his Grande Allée. Though some observers believe the purple flowers may have been tender cinerarias grown to bud-stage in pots and then transferred out-side from his greenhouse, the same effect is certainly possible

This corner of the Clos Normand is filled in autumn with the blues, pinks, and mauves of New England asters.

using any number of hardy dwarf asters, such as 'Professor Kippenberg'.

Monet grew and painted many kinds of chrysanthemums, including those we know today as bedding chrysanthemums, or cushion mums. In some of Monet's paintings it seems as if he picked an entire plant to make an instant bouquet. In North America care should be taken to choose varieties that will over-winter, since not all chrysanthemums sold in late summer and autumn for bedding are sufficiently hardy to survive severe winters. A particularly fine, extremely hardy family of cushion chrysanthemums are the 'Prophets', developed by Yoder Brothers of Ohio. Many are semidouble and daisy-flowered, and they come in a full range of russet colors. These blooms are a perfect garden complement to the changing leaf colors of deciduous trees.

A curtain of pink crab apple blossoms veils a view of Monet's Clos Normand flower garden.

The football and spider chrysanthemums featured in Monet's painting *Chrysanthemums* (1897), were most probably grown in his greenhouse, since they are tender plants not easily cultivated outdoors. An archival photograph of Monet in his first studio, before his greenhouse was built, shows what appear to be pots of football and spider chrysanthemums occupying studio space close to a picture window, so it is natural to assume that when his greenhouse was built he grew them under glass.

CHERRIES AND CRAB APPLES

All the Impressionist painters thrilled to see orchard trees in bloom, no matter how fleeting their flowering display. When Monet first moved to Giverny he was surrounded by apple and plum orchards and he painted them ardently, sometimes with his family picnicking under their blossoming canopy. Monet preferred to see his cherries and crab apples backlit by the sun, when the translucent white and pale pink petals were almost dazzling in their brightness. In the Clos Normand today, an assortment of varieties is planted to provide shade near the house and to break up the long parallel flower beds. A pair of old Japanese crab apples (*Malus floribunda*), planted by Monet, still survives near the porch. Specimens of 'Kwanzan' Japanese flowering cherry (*Prunus serrulata* 'Kwanzan')—with their powder pink pompon flowers—have replaced varieties planted by Monet. Today, a host of improved cultivars are available to gardeners, especially weeping forms of cherry, such as *Prunus subhirtella* 'Pendula'. There are also varieties of crab apples, such as 'Donald Wyeman', that are resistant to fire blight and which produce an avalanche of red, orange, or yellow berries in autumn.

CLEMATIS

Wild, white-flowered *Clematis montana* and its light pink cultivar 'Rubens' were so dear to Monet as flowering vines that he built special metal frames on which to grow them. The frames were high enough to walk under with ease, and allowed the star-shaped flowers of the clematis to dangle attractively. Monet maintained a large collection of clematis, which most likely included 'Nelly Moser', since Moser & Fils, the nursery that introduced the cultivar in 1897, was one of Monet's favorite sources for plants. 'Nelly Moser' is a large carmine and white bicolor, and remains a popular clematis cultivar today. The large, purple-blue 'Jackman' is another popular cultivar, developed in England a little earlier than 'Nelly Moser'. Monet liked to plant his clematis to twine through climbing roses, a classic combination that still inspires gardeners of every taste and experience level.

Clematis trained on an arbor, produces a lace curtain effect above a pink, blue, and white color harmony.

COLTSFOOT

Commonly called Japanese coltsfoot or Japanese butterbur, this wonderful, hardy, streamside perennial is botanically known as *Petasites japonicus*. It is valued more for its dramatic, heart-shaped, velvety leaves than for its lime green cones of daisylike flowers that appear in early spring before the leaves. Monet liked to contrast its large rounded foliage with leaves of contrasting textures and shapes, like those of irises, bamboo, daylilies, and agapanthus. Coltsfoot is invaluable for its tolerance of of boggy conditions, and it is a good plant to consider for tapestry garden effects, where the emphasis on leaf colors, textures, and shapes is important.

COSMOS

Annual cosmos grows easily from seed. *Cosmos bipinnatus* is available in red, pink, and white, while *C. sulphureus* comes in shades of yellow and orange. Monet liked cosmos for its daisylike flowers and for the plants' ability to grow as tall as his tuberous dahlias and sunflowers. Also, cosmos petals have a wonderful translucent quality when backlit by the sun.

In recent years plant breeders have developed a number of bicolored cosmos cultivars, which the gardeners at Giverny grow today. Of particular value is a cultivar known as 'Candy Stripe', which has petals that are streaked as if they were painted. The flowers create a distinctive glittering effect against feathery foliage.

DAFFODILS

In spring Monet's garden explodes with the colors of daffodils (*Narcissus* spp.) and early-blooming shrubs such as flowering currant and yellow Spanish broom, plus small flowering trees such as ornamental cherries and crab apples. Archival photographs show that Monet planted daffodils wherever he could find a bare spot. He especially liked to arrange them as islands of color on his lawn and in brilliant ribbons along the path that encircles his pond.

Above: *Japanese coltsfoot, or butterbur (*Petasites japonicus*) dips its bold, heart-shaped leaves into Monet's pond.* **Right:** *Pink cosmos adds a shimmering effect to the Clos Normand when its transparent flowers are backlit by the sun.* **Opposite:** *Fragrant daffodils appear as a brush stroke of color along one of Monet's plante bands. In the background is a gardener's cottage painted to match the main house.*

Today, the gardeners at Giverny favor the sensational large-cupped hybrid daffodil 'Professor Einstein' for its pristine white petals and wide, ruffled deep-orange trumpet. The flowers start off standing erect, then tend to flop over into the pathways, softening their hard lines. Also, 'Professor Einstein' is the preferred cultivar for planting through turf. To do this yourself, simply roll back several feet of sod in autumn (first cutting the edges of the area to be rolled with a flat-edged spade); add humus to the soil in the form of compost or peat; plant the bulbs about 6 inches (15 centimeters) deep from the base of the bulb; then roll back the turf. Daffodils are strong enough to penetrate grass roots and flower spectacularly. (Do be sure not to mow your lawn until the daffodil leaves have completely dried, or the bulb will not have gained enough strength to flower again the next year.)

Other favorite daffodils are the highly fragrant cluster-flowered kinds, also known as 'Tazetta' hybrids, particularly the cultivars 'Cragford' and 'Geranium'.

DAHLIAS

French and Dutch plant breeders pioneered a breeding program that has produced an amazing assortment of dahlia flower sizes and shapes, most of them with rounded petals (called "formal decorative" in dahlia circles) or sharply quilled petals (called "cactus-flowered"). Grown from tubers and indigenous to Mexico, dahlias were an important component of Monet's late-summer and autumn flower displays. It's easy to understand Monet's fondness for these flowers when you behold some of the large-flowered varieties, which grow to a spectacular 12 feet (3.6 meters) before frost ends their stupendous display.

An early book on Monet's garden claims that the source of Monet's dahlias was "a leading dahlia breeder, Etoile de Dijon." However, 'Etoile de Dijon' is not the name of a nursery, but rather the name of a distinctive single-flowered dahlia cultivar—its unusual curled petals created a singular star shape that Monet greatly admired. Unfortunately, the variety seems to have been lost to cultivation since Monet's day, but another favorite old cultivar, 'Bishop of Llandaff', is still widely available, sometimes sold as 'The Bishop' or 'Japanese Bishop'. In addition to a bright scarlet-red, daisylike flower, it has lustrous bronze foliage that enlivens the monotonous greens of flower borders. 'Bishop of Llandaff' blooms continuously from early summer to autumn frost.

Many of the dahlias grown in Monet's garden today are "dinner-plate" dahlias with individual blooms that can measure 10 inches (25.5 centimeters) across. Some of these are bicolored, and are especially favored for the shimmering quality they contribute. Note that the brittle, hollow stems of dahlias are easily damaged, and the large-flowered kinds in particular can become top-heavy, so staking of the large-flowered cultivars is essential.

Decorative orange dahlias billow out from a mixed border in the Clos Normand.

A mass of red geraniums in one of the island beds close to the house provides a dramatic red and green color harmony, in contrast to potted tree-form marguerite daisies.

GERANIUMS

Bedding geraniums (*Geranium* spp.) would seem to be a curious choice for Impressionist painters to have identified as a favorite flower, since they were as common for carpet bedding in parks and public gardens then as they are today. But it was not only Monet who admired them; both Caillebotte and Cézanne planted and painted geraniums. In a letter to his sister, van Gogh suggested using geraniums to create a red and green color harmony, citing particularly their "vigorous green leaves." The brown zone found on many geranium varieties was considered an important attribute, as it made the foliage appear darker than leaves that were plain green. Rose pink and blood red were Monet's favorite geranium flower colors.

In Monet's day, bedding geraniums were propagated mainly from cuttings, since that was considered the only way to get precisely the colors you wanted. Today, however, plant breeders have made geraniums easy to grow from seed, and they will bloom true to color in as little as eighty days. However, I doubt Monet would use the new seed-grown varieties. They have the advantage of blooming nonstop, long after cutting varieties have exhausted themselves, but the flower heads are comparatively delicate and shatter easily after rain. When one looks at archival photographs of Monet standing proudly beside his beds of geraniums grown from cuttings, one realizes it was the size and substance of bloom and the heavy, feltlike foliage that pleased him.

GLADIOLUS

Growing man-high, these slender flowering bulbs stand out like exclamation points in the garden, and that is exactly what Monet wanted of them. He planted the common florist gladiolus, and favored the hot colors, especially orange, scarlet, and crimson. Usually massed in island beds, the gladiolus were sometimes underplanted with a groundcover of geraniums.

Monet's painting *Gladioli* (1876) offers a glimpse at the way he planted these flowers, with the gladiolus grouped at the center of an island bed rimmed with red geraniums and underplanted with blue and black violas.

Above Left: *Monet favored fiery red and orange gladiolus for hot color combinations.* **Above Right:** *Monet preferred hollyhocks of the old-fashioned single-flowered type, probably because the cup-shaped flowers reflected light better than the double-flowered varieties.*

HOLLYHOCKS

M onet valued plants that could grow tall and bushy, and wed his low-growing varieties with tall-growing plants or flowering vines strung along metal supports. If the tall plant had decorative leaves, so much the better. The holly-hock (*Alcea rosea*) combined all these attributes; it had beautiful, large, ivy-shaped leaves and spires of irides-cent flowers studded along strong stems. Although hol-lyhocks are available in both pompon (double) and single (cup-shaped) forms, Monet liked the singles best. The cupped arrange-ment of petals reflects the sunlight, shimmering like satin, and when backlit they are translucent. A note in Monet's personal accounts book lists the color sequence for seven rows of hollyhocks, reported by art historian John House: "Purple, white, red, violet, yellow, cream, and pink."

Both Caillebotte and Pissaro fed their hollyhocks well with manure, and they grew more than 15 feet (4.6 meters) high. A specimen in Pissaro's garden even towers above the roof of his house in one of his paintings, but Monet seems to have been quite satisfied when they stayed within bounds at 6 feet (1.8 meters) high.

'Hidcote' lavender has deep violet-blue coloring—here the plants form a semicircular hedge around one of Monet's benches in a part of the property that now houses art students. The pale blue variety 'Munstead' is better when a misty effect is desired.

LAVENDER

I n summer, some of the flower beds in the Clos Normand are planted with English lavender (*Lavandula angustifolia*). Lavender forms cushions of pastel purple-blue flowers that are highly fragrant, and when plants are spaced close together they create a hedge effect. Lavender's greatest value in the landscape is in producing a misty appearance. This effect is more pronounced in the older, pale blue varieties like 'Munstead', rather than the newer dark violet-blues like 'Hidcote'. Also, there is now a large, bushy hybrid—called *Lavandula × intermedia* 'Grosso'—which is widely cultivated in Provence for its billowing, cloudlike effect.

LILACS

Monet's garden at Argenteuil, his first spacious country garden, had a grove of old lilacs (*Syringa vulgaris*) that formed a bower. Monet noted how the lilac blossoms changed color according to whether sunlight was streaming

A beautiful specimen French hybrid lilac lifts its billowing form above the plante bands *in the Clos Normand in mid-May.*

down or more muted, as on an overcast day. The lilacs were his first experiment at painting the same subject in different lighting situations. His painting *Under the Lilacs* (1873) depicts the bushes in a flood of light. It shows the sinuous trunks of the largest of his lilacs forming a billowing floral canopy, with two women sitting beneath in its cool shade. A second painting shows the same scene in diffused light, under a high cloud cover.

Another important lilaclike tree in Monet's garden is tamarix (*Tamarix ramosissima*), which produces a billowing mass of pink flowers, creating a misty appearance when seen from a distance.

LILIES

Judging from archival photographs, a favorite early planting scheme of Monet's featured the tall, funnel-shaped, white blossoms of Madonna lilies (*Lilium candidum*) paired with blue delphiniums. Later, Clemenceau declared that the gold-banded lily (*Lilium auratum*) was Monet's favorite flower. This large Japanese species is predominantly white, but is spotted with crimson and features a yellow strip on each petal segment. Monet was much impressed by a painting of these lilies by his friend the expatriate American painter John Singer Sargent. In England, Sargent labored for more than a year over a painting entitled *Carnation, Lily, Lily Rose* (1885), which shows two children in a garden at dusk, playing with Chinese lanterns among clumps of gold-banded lilies. Candles illuminate the lanterns, and a waning sun backlights the white lilies. The painting redeemed Sargent's reputation following a period of critical failure, and seems to have influenced Monet to add the highly fragrant gold-banded lily to his plant palette. He also grew many in pots.

Today, the true *L. auratum* is considered somewhat temperamental, but the cultivar 'Platyphyllum' is more vigorous and disease resistant. Its fragrant flowers are even larger than those of the species.

In recent years, tremendous strides have been made with lilies, largely as a result of the pioneering work of the late Jan de Graaff. One of de Graaff's most important introductions

Oriental hybrid lilies impressed Monet because of the translucent quality of their petals. This beautiful lily is called 'Auratum'.

was the 'Mid-Century' strain of Asiatic hybrid lilies, the easiest of all garden lilies to grow in sun or light shade. Although they were not available in Monet's time, the gardeners at Giverny today use the red, yellow, and orange cultivars extensively to create spectacular hot color beds. The lilies are usually planted together with yellow loosestrife, yellow yarrow, and annual rudbeckias.

MORNING GLORIES

Vigorous, fast-growing, annual morning glories (*Ipomoea* spp.) were important for Monet because they bloomed profusely in summer and autumn, when good blues are scarce. Monet found blue morning glories invaluable, for they added the color of the sky to his greenery. Moreover, the long, slender vines are capable of twining through other plants. He partnered blue morning glories with golden sunflowers, yellow roses, and orange climbing nasturtiums. Morning glories also come in a range of pinks and purples, as well as white.

NASTURTIUMS

Monet collected several kinds of nasturtiums (*Tropaeolum* spp.), and especially admired their ability to vine vertically or horizontally. In recent years plant breeders have concentrated their efforts on developing dwarf, compact, bushy varieties, and the vining nasturtiums have become rather scarce, though they may still be found in seed catalogs. Annual nasturtiums produce rapidly growing vines up to 12 feet (3.7 meters) high. Monet trained nasturtiums to weave in and out of other tall or climbing plants, such as sunflowers and morning glories. He planted them on opposite sides of his Grande

PERFECT PARTNERS

MONET ESPECIALLY LIKED TO PLANT BLUE ANNUAL MORNING GLORIES IN PROXIMITY TO YELLOW AND ORANGE FLOWERS, SUCH AS SUNFLOWERS. THIS IS AN EASY PLANT PARTNERSHIP TO ORCHESTRATE SINCE BOTH SUNFLOWERS AND MORNING GLORIES ARE ANNUALS, GROW QUICKLY FROM DIRECT-SOWN SEEDS, AND FLOWER OVER A LONG PERIOD BEGINNING IN MIDSUMMER.

Nasturtiums nod in company with pink geraniums and white alyssum. Monet used vining nasturtiums in orange, red, and yellow to complete the effect of a floral tunnel along his Grande Allée.

Allée so their parasols of foliage would creep across the ground and almost meet in the middle of the broad path.

Monet liked an annual nasturtium known today as 'Empress of India', which he grew up tripods that were evenly spaced among his beds of geraniums. This nasturtium sports bronze foliage and dark crimson flowers. Visitors to Monet's garden during his lifetime described a crimson perennial nasturtium, which he threaded through iron fencing; this was undoubtedly the flame nasturtium (*Tropaeolum speciosum*).

PANSIES

For generations, the Roggli family in Switzerland has produced the finest pansies (*Viola* spp.) the world has ever known. Pansies are native to the Swiss Alps, and the large-flowered hybrids known as Swiss Giants are similar to the pansies Monet grew. Of particular appeal to Monet were the blotched varieties, since the black markings at the center of the pansy

PERFECT PARTNERS

PANSIES (*Viola* SPP.) HAVE EXTENSIVE COLOR RANGES, AND MANY OF THE HUES ARE COMPLETE WITH TOUCHES OF MAROON OR BLACK, WHICH HELPS TO CREATE A GLITTERING EFFECT. HERE, 'HELEN MOUNT' PANSIES—WITH THEIR MAROON-FLECKED OF PETAL TIPS—MIX BEAUTIFULLY WITH BLUE FORGET-ME-NOTS AND YELLOW ALYSSUM.

flower help give it a shimmering appearance, especially when there are plenty of white pansies with black faces. Planted together, blotched pansies convey the impression of flickering brush strokes on a canvas.

Several other distinct advantages of pansies are early flowering, a long-lasting flower display, and tolerance of shade. Though the color range is uncommonly wide—it includes shades of blue, red, and yellow—the most effective plantings separate the colors into hot colors (orange, apricot, yellow, and reds) and cool colors (blue, purple, mauve, and pale pink). Try planting blue, purple, mauve, and pale pink pansies along a woodland path or in a part of the garden that produces dappled shade, and see how well these colors improve a shady situation.

Pansies are closely related to smaller-flowered violas, which Monet also grew. He particularly liked combinations of blue and black violas underplanted in beds of gladiolus.

PENSTEMONS AND SALVIAS

We know that Monet liked hardy penstemons (*Penstemon* spp.) planted liberally throughout his garden because of reports by visitors, notably botanist Georges Truffaut, who wrote, "...the distinctive flower of Claude Monet's garden is the penstemon. Any gardener seeing the Giverny penstemons would want to grow some."

Two species, *Penstemon barbatus* and *P. hartwegii*, have loose stems of tubular red flowers that look like flecks of red paint. There are also white varieties that can add a glittering appearance to borders. Today at Giverny, while the gardeners still plant both white and red penstemon, they use a look-alike scarlet sage (*Salvia coccinea*), notably the annual cultivar 'Lady in Red', more often. This recent introduction to the world of bedding annuals has the advantage of looking like a penstemon, but it is everblooming. Like old-fashioned penstemons, its presence does not block other flowers planted behind it, and it does not have the density of bloom that makes the more familiar red salvia *S. splendens* difficult to use in mixed borders. One year, however, for the sheer thrill of seeing a dramatic red, green, and silver combination in the dianthus-edged island beds below his porch, Monet is said to have planted *S. splendens*. Some observers wondered whatever could have possessed him to use such a garish common bedding plant. He probably chose this salvia because its shade of red is unique for its purity and brilliance, and for its wide, serrated green leaves, which highlight the color magnificently. What did it matter if a plant was common? For Monet, it was the color that was crucial.

The perpetual-flowering perennial sage 'Lady in Red' has largely replaced penstemons in Monet's restored garden because its looks so much like penstemon but has a longer flowering display.

PEONIES

Monet grew both the woody, shrublike tree peony (*Paeonia suffruticosa*) and the easier-to-grow herbaceous perennial peony, *P. lactiflora* and hybrids. His tree peonies were mostly planted in clearings around his water garden. Purchased from specialist nurseries in Japan, Monet acquired what was undoubtedly the most valuable collection in France, some of the flowers measuring more than a foot (30 centimeters) across. Today, tree peonies are not as prominent a feature of the water garden because the shores of the pond are shadier and more crowded. Still, a few of the smaller yellow and apricot varieties are represented.

Much more common today at Giverny are the herbaceous peonies, which Monet acquired from France's leading peony breeder, La Maison Crousse, in Nancy. The Crousse collection was started by the Empress Josephine and spawned many exceptional hybrids still popular today, including the sensational rosy red 'Felix Crousse', still grown at Giverny. In June there is no more glorious sight than the presence of big, bold clumps of white, pink, and rosy red peonies blooming with blue bearded irises and red Oriental poppies.

In his powerful painting *Peonies* (1910), Monet captures the brilliant pink tones of herbaceous peonies beneath a lightly shaded canopy that shelters the plants from heavy rains, which can easily shatter the petals.

PERFECT PARTNERS

ROSY PINK HERBACEOUS PEONIES LOOK FABULOUS IN COMPANY WITH PINK TREE FORM ROSES AND RED ORIENTAL POPPIES. NOTE, TOO, THE WAY THE AIRY WHITE FLOWERS OF DAME'S ROCKET ARE SPRINKLED LIBERALLY THROUGHOUT THE BEDS TO CREATE THE SENSATION OF SHIMMER THAT VISITORS FIND VISUALLY UPLIFTING.

POPPIES

An indication of Monet's passion for poppies can be found in a letter to an art dealer, Maurice Joubert: "Thank you for having thought of me for the Hokusai flowers. You don't mention the poppies, and that is the important one, for I already have the iris, the chrysanthemums, the peonies, and the convolvulus."

Red European corn poppies (*Papaver commutatum*) grew wild in fallow fields all around Giverny, and Monet brought these cheerful annuals into his garden, allowing them to seed into any bare patch of soil among his hybrids. Another favorite annual poppy was the California poppy (*Eschscholzia californica*), because its petals have a satiny sheen and the orange tones go well with nasturtiums. Monet also adored the plate-size blooms of Oriental poppies (*Papaver orientale*), for they produced flaming discordant notes among his bearded irises, which bloomed at the same time.

Two poppies that have found wide acceptance among the gardeners today at Giverny are *P. commutatum* 'Lady Bird', which has crimson petals and handsome black petal markings, and *P. orientale* 'Turkin Louise', which has fringed petal edges.

ROSES

Monet adored roses, and he planted both old garden roses and modern roses such as hybrid teas. Shrub roses, climbers, and standard roses are among the most prominent flowers in the Clos Normand (see page 91).

'Mermaid', a thorny, yellow, single-flowered climber with a large saucer shape, was one of Monet's favorites. This rose also has distinctive foliage, which is almost bright red in its juvenile form, and later turns a rich, lustrous dark green.

'Nevada', a large, single-flowered white hybrid shrub rose, is grown today along the banks of the pond at Giverny, its long arching canes allowed to bow forward and dip into the surface of the water. The individual blooms are the size of saucers and hug the canes so generously they seem like stars in a galaxy, echoing the sparkles of sunlight on the water.

'American Pillar' is an important feature of the high rose arch that covers the boat dock, its single carmine flowers falling like a curtain in large clusters from canes that can exceed 20 feet (6 meters). Monet discovered 'American Pillar' in the 1908 mail-order catalog of Conard and Jones, a nursery located in West Grove, Pennsylvania.

'The Fairy'—a soft pink polyanthus rose—was first introduced in 1932. Displaying buttonlike flowers in dense

Oriental poppies provide a strong primary color contrast among blue and yellow bearded irises in the Clos Normand.

clusters, it is a favorite today in the garden at Giverny for grafting as a tree form, since it is rarely without flowers from early summer to autumn frost. It contrasts magnificently with blue lavender.

'Paul's Scarlet', another of Monet's cherished roses, is an incredibly free-flowering, scarlet-red rose with vigorous canes. In June the blooms are often so dense that they almost completely hide the foliage.

Monet planted clematis to grow in among his climbing roses, and he paired yellow roses with blue flowers such as morning glories and larkspur.

SPIDER FLOWERS

Botanically known as *Cleome hasslerana*, spider flowers are tall-growing tender annuals. They are difficult to grow in small spaces, since they may stand 5 feet (1.5 meters) tall by the end of the season, and their long, slender lengths of stem and foliage can look rather ungainly. But in a large garden spider flowers rise above low-growing, bushier plants in an impressive display. Their spidery flower heads, usually bicolored pink and white, produce an appealing shimmer, especially when the flowers are backlit.

Left: *Creamy yellow petals and golden stamens made the single-flowered 'Mermaid' rose a favorite in the Clos Normand.*
Right: *Cool-colored spider flowers partnered with New England asters produce a glittering effect in the autumn landscape.*

SUNFLOWERS

Monet grew many sunflowers (*Helianthus* spp.), both annual and perennial types. Early on he took a great liking to the tall, giant-flowered annual 'Mammoth Russian', painting masses of them towering above his garden, against a blue sky at Vétheuil. He paired these sunflowers with gladiolus and nasturtiums for a stunning hot color combination.

Monet also painted annual sunflowers in a beautiful still life arrangement. A letter from van Gogh to his brother explains the impact this painting had on him: "Gauguin was telling me the other day that he had seen a picture by Claude Monet of sunflowers in a large Japanese vase, very fine—but he likes mine better. I don't agree."

At Giverny, Monet added many perennial sunflowers to his garden, especially the late-flowering dark-eyed sunflower (*Helianthus atrorubens*). This species is similar to Jerusalem artichoke (*H. tuberosus*), which is more widely available in North America. Monet planted these flowers so they lifted their heads above cushions of blue New England asters, achieving his famous gold and sapphire color harmony.

TULIPS

Monet traveled twice to Holland to paint the bulb fields in spring. Sometimes he painted them with a windmill, as in *Tulip Fields in Holland* (1886), or with a thatched cottage in the background, as in *Tulip Fields* (1886). He expressed some frustration at painting these "vast fields of open flowers," stating that they were "enough to drive the poor painter mad, for it cannot be rendered with our poor colors."

Discussing his visits to Holland, Monet told the Duc de Trévise, "Many times one is lucky enough to have the same light, as in Holland.... Tulips are beautiful but they are impossible to render. When I saw them I said to myself that they could not be painted. And then, for twelve days running I had pretty much the same weather. What luck! You don't like fields of tulips? You think they are too uniform? I love them."

Actually, none of Monet's tulip field paintings are of a single, uniform color, but of numerous colors in blocks, presenting a patchwork of color.

After a tour of the Clos Normand, the Duc de Trévise noted a heavy use of tulips and penned the following recollection: "The flowers are arranged impeccably; on the edge of a path aubretias form a blue border that looks painted in a solid color, while in the middle of the square flower beds tulips,

Above: *Perennial sunflowers* (Helianthus atrorubens) *are a valuable late-flowering feature of Monet's plante bands.* **Opposite:** *Bicolored Rembrandt tulips and English wall-flowers create a dazzling hot color scheme at the bottom of Monet's flower garden.*

selected from the finest catalogs from Holland and England, are scattered seemingly at random, but actually united by shades as tenuous as feeling."

Monet's favorite tulips were the lily-flowered types with pointed petals; he loved the streaked Rembrandts with their flaming petals and the single-flowered cottage tulips known as Darwins, especially the bicolors. The lily-flowered group is noted for the purest colors in tulips, particularly yellow and pink. The bicoloring in the cottage tulips and the Rembrandts helps create a shimmering sensation, especially when one of the two colors is white.

VERBASCUM

This wayside plant grows as a weed throughout France, and the species commonly called mullein (*Verbascum thapsus*) has also made itself at home in North America. Monet admired its large, silvery leaves and poker-straight flower spike, which could reach a height of 8 feet (2.4 meters). No matter that it flowered sparsely compared to other verbascums, he appreciated mullein's sculptural quality and its dark silhouette against the sky when backlit.

WALLFLOWERS

Monet used English wallflowers (*Cheiranthus cheiri*), an important spring-flowering biennial, for their rich range of hot colors. Monet used English wallflowers as the primary component of his sunset borders, and planted red columbine among them to add a more intense red and for extra height. Rosy red crab apples mark the beginning and end of the sunset beds, so that when the crab apples are in full flower the scorching tones of the sinking sun seem to set all the colors aflame.

The Giverny gardeners today, however, plant the Siberian wallflower (*Erysimum hieraciifolium*) just as often as the English type. The cultivars 'Yellow Bedder' and 'Orange Bedder' offer a purity of yellow and orange unequaled among the English wallflowers.

WATER LILIES

Water lilies (*Nymphaea* spp.) are perhaps the most famous of the flowers Monet grew and painted. All of his water lilies were obtained from the premier hybridizer Joseph Bory Latour-Marliac, and he experimented with most of Marliac's water lilies at one time or another (see page 74). In addition to fragrant white water lilies, Monet grew these flowers in shades of pink, red, orange, and yellow.

*Monet treasured verbascums (*Verbascum chaixi* is shown here) for their generous spiky flowers and dark green, velvety leaves.*

'Attraction' in a rich, rosy red; 'Chromatella' in bright yellow; the orange 'Comanche'; and blush pink 'Caroliniana' were all planted by Monet.

These are all hardy cultivars, capable of surviving harsh winters providing that their roots remain below the ice line. Monet tried tropicals, which must be taken indoors during freezing weather, but he found the pond water too cold for them, even in summer. He did have a small planting of tropical water lilies in tubs in his greenhouse, however.

Water lilies are particularly beautiful when viewed between curtains of weeping willow foliage. The gardeners at Giverny today echo the water lily colors on the adjacent banks—yellow flag irises match the iridescent yellow 'Chromatella', dark red astilbes are planted near red 'Escarboucle', and frothy pink meadowfoam matches the pale pink of 'Caroliniana'. Red water lily cultivars are also exquisite when contrasted with the dark blues of Japanese irises.

WISTERIA

Monet grew both purple and white wisteria in his gardens at Giverny (see page 67). Threaded through the arching canopy that covers the Japanese bridge, the wisteria creates a magnificent effect. The purple wisteria bloomed first, with the white overlapping a bit but extending bloom for several more weeks.

Wisteria is an extremely aggressive woody vine that demands a strong support. If you plant wisteria, take care to thin it well if the branches are supported by wood, such as bridge railings or a wooden arbor. Too dense a vine canopy will quickly cause the wood supports to rot.

Monet used a wide range of plants in his gardens at Giverny, and even more are grown there today, capturing the spirit of Monet's original plantings if not remaining faithful to his exact plant palette. By choosing cultivars Monet admired and planted for the color of their flowers, textures of their leaves, translucence of their petals, or their sculptural forms, you can capture in your own backyard the essence of the painter's exquisite garden.

PERFECT PARTNERS

SIBERIAN WALLFLOWER 'YELLOW BEDDER' MASSED IN FRONT OF A TAMARISK TREE DISPLAYING ITS MISTY PINK FLOWERS.

CONCLUSION

"It is essential to make the pilgrimage to the flowered sanctuary of Giverny, the better to understand the master, to grasp the sources of his inspiration, and to imagine his still living among us."

—GERALD VAN DER KEMP, CURATOR OF THE MONET MUSEUM

It is important to realize that Monet was no armchair gardener, directing others to do his bidding. Novelist Octave Mirbeau remembered seeing him "in shirtsleeves, his hands black with soil, his face tanned by the sun, happy to be planting seeds." To another visitor, Monet declared, "I dug, planted, weeded myself, in the evenings the children watered." Even when he could afford an experienced head gardener and a crew of undergardeners Monet would get involved in every aspect of the daily routine, leaving detailed notes before departing on a trip. A typical note to his head gardener, reminds his gardener Breuil:

"More than anything I must have flowers, always, always . . . ." Monet is buried in the church cemetery at Giverny. There he lies, still surrounded by flowers, beside his second wife, Alice, whom he outlived by fifteen years.

"sow 300 pots of Poppies—60 Sweet Peas—around 60 pots white Agremony (feverfew)—30 yellow Agremony—Blue Sage—blue Water lilies in beds—Dahlias—Iris kaempferi. From the 15th to the 25th, lay the dahlias down to root; plant those with shoots before I get back. Don't forget the lily bulbs. Should the Japanese peonies arrive plant them immediately if the weather permits, taking care initially to protect buds from the cold, as much as from the heat of the sun. Get down to pruning: rose trees not too long, except for the thorny varieties."

Monet, the master painter and the master gardener, leaves us in no doubt that he was in total control of his environment. His presence can still be strongly felt in his restored garden today, even when it is thronged with tourists. His gravesite is within walking distance of the garden, up a steep flight of steps at the entrance to the local church. It features a large stone cross, the base of which is almost always decorated with live potted plants.

It would be wonderful if we could transport ourselves briefly back in time to the years when Monet was alive and gardening at Giverny. Imagine sitting down with Monet and his family at lunch, in their comfortable yellow dining room, watching the master of the household carve a goose, comment on the flavor of his home-grown vegetables, test the red wine, and pass judgment on cheeses and the day's work. He would likely discuss gardening and decide a time to tour the garden.

To satisfy my curiosity, I would ask about the most important lessons he learned from the master plantsman Caillebotte and his American neighbor, Lilla Cabot Perry. What, if anything, did he learn from the writings of Gertrude Jekyll, and did they ever meet?

Monet collected works of other great Impressionists, especially Renoir, Pissaro, and Cézanne. And he is said to have admired van Gogh's work. Van Gogh's brother, Theo, was one of Monet's dealers, but Monet never acquired a painting of van Gogh's. I would like to know why. What would Monet think of van Gogh's current status as the world's most highly rated artist?

I have returned many times to Honfleur, the beautiful channel port where Monet lived during the early days of his career, and where he painted many seaside motifs. From Honfleur I have traveled the entire length of the spectacular coast road from Le Havre to Dieppe, walking sections of cliffs where Monet painted numerous clifftop meadows and seascapes. I have stood transfixed at the spectacular rock formations at Etretat, where Monet once broke his leg walking across slippery rocks. These are spiritual places, and they make us feel good to be alive. But still the most uplifting experience of all is to return to the intimacy of Monet's cultivated gardens and see how he distilled so many visual pleasures gleaned from the natural world into a few sloping acres beyond his door.

VISITING MONET'S GARDEN

Giverny is a little over 30 miles (50 kilometers) from Paris off the A13 motorway north. The closest railway station is Vernon, a one-hour train ride from the Gare Saint Lazare in Paris. There are also tour buses that run day trips from Paris to Monet's garden. The garden is open from April 1 through October 31, 10 A.M. to 6 P.M. daily, except Mondays, when it is open only to painters with appointments and to VIPs.

A good place to stay in the area is the Hotel d'Evreux, in the center of Vernon. The accommodations are comfortable and the restaurant is excellent. Monet himself frequently stayed in the hotel, and dined there with Renoir.

While visiting Monet's garden, consider a visit to the American Museum, which is a short walk away through the village. Founded by American art patrons Judith and Daniel Terra, it features works by American Impressionist artists who descended on Giverny in droves when the genius of Monet's work became known in the United States.

There are several particularly beautiful gardens to see in the Normandy countryside. Clos Coudray, featuring English-style gardens around a beautiful restored thatched cottage, is about an hour's drive just north of Rouen. Parc Floral de Moutiers, at Varengeville, features a residence designed by the famous British architect Sir Edwin Lutyens for a collector of Impressionist art, Guillaime Mallet, and a garden with elements designed by Gertrude Jekyll. A few miles south is Le Vasterival, the superb woodland property of Princess Sturdza, whose garden features many of the design principles espoused by Gertrude Jekyll in her book *Water & Woodland*; nearby are cliff walks to places where Monet painted forty-four canvases.

ABOUT THE AUTHOR

Derek Fell is a prolific writer and photographer who specializes in recording the romantic qualities of gardens. He lives in Bucks County, Pennsylvania, at historic Cedaridge Farm, where he cultivates extensive award-winning flower and vegetable gardens. His work is featured in *Architectural Digest, Hemispheres, Woman's Day, Gardens Illustrated,* and *Fine Gardening* magazines. He also hosts a popular television garden show for the QVC cable channel, "Step-by-Step Gardening."

Fell has lectured on photography and the gardens of the great Impressionist painters at numerous art museums, including the Smithsonian Institution, the Barnes Foundation, the Philadelphia Museum of Art, the Denver Art Museum, the Walters Art Gallery (Baltimore), the Dixon Art Gallery (Nashville), and the Renoir Foundation. Fell's photography is sold in signed editions, and his photographic art poster, *Monet's Bridge* (Portal), is displayed and sold at the Monet Museum, Giverny, France. Another photograph, *Monet's Roses,* has been added to the series of Contemporary American Photographers note card sets, published by Palm Press.

Born and educated in England, Derek Fell worked for seven years with Europe's largest seed house, before immigrating to the United States. After six years with Burpee Seeds, he became executive director of All-America Selections (the national seed trials) and the National Garden Bureau (an information office sponsored by the American seed industry). The author of more than 50 garden books and calendars, he has traveled throughout North America, Europe, Africa, South America, New Zealand, and Japan to document gardens. His most recent books on the Impressionist painters are *Renoir's Garden* (Simon & Schuster) and *The Impressionist Garden* (Crown).

Derek Fell has won more awards from the Garden Writers Association of America than any other garden writer. He worked as a consultant on garden design to the White House during the Ford Administration.

He is married with three children, Tina, Derek Jr., and Victoria. His wife, Carolyn, is an expert on flower arranging and a professional stylist.

Fell's property, Cedaridge Farm, has 24 theme gardens that take inspiration from the great Impressionist painters, including Monet. From April 25 through November 1 the gardens are open by appointment. For further information about visiting Cedaridge Farm, write Cedaridge Farm, Box 1, Gardenville, PA 18926.

SOURCES

Monet used a great many sources for seeds, bulbs, plants, and ornaments such as arches and planters. Below you'll find mail-order companies that supply plants and garden features that capture the spirit of the garden at Giverny.

ARBORS
Kinsman Company
River Road
Point Pleasant, PA 18950

BENCHES
The Bench Smith
PO Box 86
Warrington, PA 18976

DAHLIAS
Swan Island Dahlias
PO Box 800
Canby, OR 97013

IRISES
Schreiners Iris Gardens
3625 Quinaby Road NE
Salem, OR 97303

LILIES
Rex Bulb Farms
2568 Washington Street
Port Townsend, WA 98368

PEONIES
Klehm Nursery
197 Penny Road
South Barrington, IL 60010

ROSES
Conard-Pyle Company
228 School House Road
West Grove, PA 19390

SEEDS
Thompson & Morgan
Box 1308
Jackson, NJ 08527

TULIPS
Dutch Gardens
PO Box 200
Adelphia, NJ 07710

WATER LILIES
Lilypons Water Gardens
Box 10
Buckeystown, MD 21717

AUSTRALIA
Country Farm Perennials
RSD Laings Road
Nayook VIC 3821

Cox's Nursery
RMB 216 Oaks Road
Thrilmere NSW 2572

Honeysuckle Cottage Nursery
Lot 35 Bowen Mountain Road
Bowen Mountain via Grosevale
NSW 2753

Swan Bros Pty Ltd
490 Galston Road
Dural NSW 2158

CANADA
Corn Hill Nursery Ltd.
RR 5
Petitcodiac
NB EOA 2HO

Ferncliff Gardens
SS 1
Mission, British Columbia
V2V 5V6

McFayden Seed Co. Ltd.
Box 1800
Brandon, Manitoba
R7A 6N4

Stirling Perennials
RR 1
Morpeth, Ontario
N0P 1X0

INDEX

AGAPANTHUS, 32, 71, 118, *118*, 119
ARBORS, 57
Artist's Garden at Vétheuil (MONET), 58, *59*
Artist's Studio Overlooking the Garden, Spring (CAILLEBOTTE), 31
ASTERS, 93, 119–120
    NEW ENGLAND, 43, 58, 88, 93, *119*
ASTILBE, 25, 139
AUBRETIA, 20, 85
AZALEA, 25, 73, 77, *102*, 110

BAMBOO, 25, 104
BEETS, 100–101
BELLIS, FLORENCE, 17
BENCHES, *50–51*, 52–53, *52*, *53*
Bend in the River Epte (MONET), 14
BIRCH, RIVER, 25, 113
BIRD FEEDERS AND BOXES, 62
BISHOP'S WEED, 34
BLACK-AND-WHITE COLOR HARMONY, 31–32, 44
BLUE
    IN SHADE, 32–33, *33*, 47
    See also COLOR HARMONIES
BLUEBELLS, 32
BLUE HOUSE, 19, *19*, 96
BOONE, VIOLET, 35
BOUDIN, EUGÈNE, 104
BRIDGES, 54–56, *54*, *56*, 67, 67–68, 70, *71*
BROWN, JOHN, 19
BUTTERFLIES, 62, 93
BUTTERFLY BUSH, 93

CAILLEBOTTE, GUSTAVE, 13, 19–20, 31, 39, 44, 53, 58, 82, 83, 85, 125, 127
CALENDULA, 43
CARPETING EFFECT, 114, *114*
Cerastium tomentosum, 26, *27*
CÉZANNE, PAUL, 13, 17, 39, 107, 125
CHAMOMILE, 32, 43
CHARD, 100, *101*
CHERRY, 114, *115*, 120–121
CHEVREUL, MICHEL-EUGÈNE, 40–41
CHRYSANTHEMUMS, 88, 93, 120
CLEMATIS, 26, 27, 29, 43, 48, 49, 57, 60, 93, *121*, *121*
CLEMENCEAU, GEORGES, 14

CLOS NORMAND, 49, 62, 80–81, 120, 128
    BEARDED IRIS IN, 90, *90*, 112, 134
    BENCHES IN, 52
    CAILLEBOTTE'S INFLUENCE ON, 83, 85
    CLEARING OF SITE, 86
    COLOR IN, 88, *88*, 93
    ENGLISH-STYLE OF, 19, 21, 70, 82
    LAYOUT OF, *20*, 22–23, 28, 85, 86, 87, 88
    ROSES IN, *91*, 91–92, 134
    WALLS OF, 60, *60*
    See also GRAND ALLÉE
COLD FRAMES, 101, *101*
COLOR
    BACKLIT, 30–31
    BICOLORED FLOWERS, 26, 28
    BRONZE FOLIAGE, 34
    PURITY, 30
    SEASONAL, 44–45, 93
    FOR SHADE, 32–33, *33*, 47, *47*
    SHIMMERING, 26, 27, 28, 29
    THEORY, 40–41
    TIERS OF, 88, *88*
COLOR HARMONIES, 70, 83
    BLACK-WHITE, 31–32, 44
    BLUE-MAUVE, 33
    BLUE-PINK, 90
    BLUE-PINK-WHITE, 21, 41, *41*, 42, 43
    COOL COLORS, 45, 46, 47, 49
    HOT COLORS, 36–37, 47, 48, 49
    ORANGE-BLUE, 43
    PINK-MAUVE, 33
    RED-GREEN-SILVER, 21, 40, 41
    YELLOW-BLUE, 21, *90*
    YELLOW-VIOLET, 43, *43*
COLTSFOOT, 25, 122, *122*
COLUMBINE, 43, 138
CONARD AND JONES, 14
CORALBELLS, 43
CORNFLOWERS, 26
COSMOS, 33, 93, 122, *122*
COTTAGE GARDEN, 70, 82
CRAB APPLE, 41, 48, 49, *111*, 112, 120, 120–121, 138
CROCUS, 86
CUP GARDEN CONCEPT, 19, 68, *69*, 70

DAFFODILS, 73, 93, 122, *123*, 124
DAHLIAS, 34, 93, 124, *124*
DAISIES, 30, 32, 33, 35, *35*, 47, 119
Dame's rocket, 43, *133*

DAVIES, BILL AND BARBARA, 17, 76
DAYLILIES, 45
DECAISNE, JOSEPH, 41
DE GRAAFF, JAN, 129
DELPHINIUM, 28
DEWHURST, WYNFORD, 21
DIANTHUS, 40, 41
DUSTY MILLER, 40

EMPRESS TREE, 113
ENGLISH-STYLE GARDEN, 19, 21, 70, 82
ESPALIERED TREES, 60, 97, 98, 99, *99*

FEVERFEW, 43
Field of Yellow Irises (MONET), 32
FIRECRACKER VINE, 57
FLAX, 43
Flowering Arches, The (MONET), 54
FORGET-ME-NOTS, 25, 26, 27, 32, 33, *33*, 42, 43, 47, *131*
FORSYTHIA, 60, *61*

GATES, 58
GEFFROY, GUSTAVE, 92, 93
GERANIUMS, 40, 41, 93, 125, 125–126
Gladioli (MONET), 92, 93, 126
GLADIOLUS, 58, 93, 126, *126*
GOLDEN CHAIN TREE, 25
GRAND ALLÉE, *11*, 13, 24, 58, *58*, *59*, 60, 86, 88, *108*
GREENBERG, CLEMENT, 24
GREENHOUSES, 62–63, *63*

HAYSTACKS NEAR GIVERNY (MONET), *105*
HOG WEED, 45
HOLLYHOCKS, 44, 93, *126*, 127
HOSCHEDÉ, JEAN-MICHEL, 13, 34
HOSTA, 25, 71
HOT COLORS, 36–37, 47, 48, 49
House at Argenteuil (MONET), 45
HYBRIDS, 34–35

IMPATIENS, 88
IMPRESSIONISM
    ARTIST'S MATERIALS AND, 38–40
    COLOR THEORY AND, 40–41
    JAPANESE INFLUENCE ON, 40

IRIS, 41
    BEARDED, 28, *28*, 32, 35, 43, 44, 46, 47, 90, 112, 134
    FLAG, 25, 32, 35, 64–65, 77, 139
    JAPANESE, 25, 71, 77, 139

JAPANESE ART, 40, 105
JAPANESE GARDEN, 19, 66–67, 70, 106
JARDIN DES PLANTES, *10*, 11, 34, 62
JEANNIOT, GEORGES, 38
JEKYLL, GERTRUDE, 17, 20–21, 41, 45, 82
JOYES, CLAIRE, 14, 19

KELWAYS NURSERIES, 34–35

LABURNUM, 109, *109*, 114
LACE-CURTAIN EFFECT, 21, 29
LADY'S MANTLE, 25
LARKSPUR, 43
LATOUR-MARLIAC NURSERY, 16, 17, 74, 75, 76
LAVENDER, 49, 93, 127, *127*–128
LEAF TUNNELS, 107, *108*, 109
LEOPARD'S BANE, 119
LIGHT AND SHADE CONTRAST, 89, 110
LILACS, 128, 128–129
LILIES, 83, 129, *129*
LOOSESTRIFE, 83
LOVE-LIES-BLEEDING, 93
LUPINE, 25

MAGPIE, THE (MONET), 31, *31*, 44, 106
MAPLE, JAPANESE, 25, 45, 64, 71, 77
MARLIAC, JOSEPH BORY LATOUR, 17, 35, 74–75, 78, 138
MEADOWFOAM, 25, 139
MEADOWSWEET, 68
METCALF, WILLARD, 19, 96–97, 97
MIRBEAU, OCTAVE, 26, 47, 51
MONET, CLAUDE
    PAINTING STYLE OF, 38, 104–106
    PHOTOGRAPHY USE BY, 39–40
    See also MONET'S GARDEN
Monet's Formal Garden (METCALF), 96–97, 97
MONET'S GARDEN
    BLUE HOUSE, 19, *19*, 96
    HAZY EFFECT IN, 49
    ILLUSION OF DISTANCE IN, 49

INFLUENCES ON, 19–21
LACE-CURTAIN EFFECT IN, 21, 29
PHILOSOPHY BEHIND, 11–12, 13, 28,
    44. *SEE ALSO* COLOR; COLOR
    HARMONIES
PINK HOUSE, 13, *18*, 19, *19*, 96
RESTORATION OF, 13–14
STRUCTURES IN, 50–63
VEGETABLE GARDEN, 13, 19, 20,
    94–95, 96–101, 97
VISITORS TO, 12–13
SEE ALSO CLOS NORMAND; PLANTS;
    WATER GARDEN
MONET'S GARDEN AT GIVERNY (MONET),
    45, *84*, *85*
MONET'S TABLE (JOYES), 19
MONET-STYLE GARDEN, 24–26, 76–77,
    88, 98
MORNING GLORIES, 43, 130, *130*
MUSHROOMS, 100

*N*ASTURTIUMS, 13, 34, 43, 47, 58, *58*,
    59, 88, 130–131, *131*
NAUDIN, CLAUDE, 41
NICOTIANA, 93
NUTT, PATRICK, 17

*O*RANGE-BLUE COLOR HARMONY, 43
ORCHARD, 114, 120–121
OSTRICH FERN, 25

*P*ANSIES, 26, 31, 32, *32*, 33, 36–37, 43,
    70, *131*, 131–132
PAUL, WILLIAM, 91
PENSTEMONS, 132
PEONIES, 25, 35, 46, 47, 90, 97, 133, *133*
PEPPERS, 100
PERRY, LILLA CABOT, 63, 67
PHLOX, *119*
PHOTOGRAPHY, PAINTING FROM, 38–40
PINK HOUSE, *18*, 19, *19*, 86, 96
PISSARO, CAMILLE, 127
PLANTERS, 60, 61, 62
PLANTS, 116–139
    BICOLORED, 28
    HEDGES OF, 97, 98
    HYBRIDS, 34–35
    FOR MONET-STYLE GARDEN, 25–26,
        88, 98

IN SHADE, 32–33
SINGLE FLOWER, 33
SOURCES FOR, 14, 17, 34–35
WITH VARIEGATED FOLIAGE, 34, *34*
VINES, 21, 29, 57, 60, 109
WILDFLOWERS, 35
SEE ALSO COLOR; COLOR HAR-
    MONIES; TREES; *SPECIFIC NAMES*
POINTILLISM, 14
POLLARDED WILLOWS, 112–113, *113*
POPPIES, 30, 32, 35, 41, 47, 90, 133,
    134, *134*
POPPIES, THE (MONET), 39
POPPY FIELD IN HOLLOW NEAR GIVERNY
    (MONET), 41
PRIMROSES, 17, *17*, 25, 73, 135
PROUST, MARCEL, 21

*R*EDBUD, 109, 114
RED-GREEN-SILVER COLOR HARMONY,
    40, 41
RENOIR, PIERRE-AUGUSTE, 13, 17, 38,
    52, 112
RHODODENDRON, 25
ROBINSON, WILLIAM, 82
ROSES, 41, 43, 45, 91–92, 104, 133,
    134–135
    CLIMBING, 14, 25, 60, 91, 110
ROSES, THE (MONET), 96

*S*AGE, 40, 41, 43, 132, *132*
SALVIA, 88, 132
SARGENT, JOHN SINGER, 129
SHADE
    COLORS, 32–33, *33*, 47, *47*
    AND LIGHT CONTRAST, 89, 110
SHIMMERING EFFECT, 26, 27, 28, 29
SILK TREE, 113
SILVER FLEECE VINE, 57
SISLEY, ALBERT, 82, 112
SISSON, FRANÇOIS THIEBAULT, 68
SKYLINE EFFECTS, 106–107
SMOKE BUSH, 49
SPIDER FLOWERS, 88, 93, 135, *135*
SQUASH, 101
SUNFLOWERS, 43, 44–45, 58, 88, 93, 119,
    130, 136, *136*
SUNRISE BORDERS, 45, 46, 47
SUNSET BORDERS, 47, 48, 49, 138

*T*AMARIX, 49, 104, 129, *139*
THOMPSON & MORGAN, 34–35
TOMATOES, 101
TOULGOUAT, JEAN-MARIE, 14, 45
TREES
    CARPETING EFFECT, 114, *114*
    CAST SHADOWS, 113
    ESPALIERED, 60, 97, 98, 99, *99*
    FRAMING, 110
    LEAF TUNNELS, 107, *108*, 109
    LINES OF, 110, *111*
    ORCHARD, 114
    POLLARDED, 112–113, *113*
    SKYLINE, *102–103*, 106, 106–107
    SEE ALSO SPECIFIC NAMES
TRELLIS, 60
TRUFFAUT, GEORGES, 13, 104
TULIPS, 26, *26*, 27, 28, 30, 36–37, 41,
    42, 90, 93, 136, *137*, 138
TUNNARD, CHRISTOPHER, 20–21
TURNER, J. M. W., 26

*V*AN DER KEMP, GERALD AND
    FLORENCE, 13, 45
VAN GOGH, VINCENT, 11, 112, 136
VARIEGATED FOLIAGE, 34, *34*
VEGETABLE GARDEN, 13, 19, 20, 94–95,
    96–101, 97
VERBASCUM, 93, 138, *138*
VERSAILLES, 52, 62
VINES, 21, 29, 57, 60, 109
VIOLAS, 132
VIRGINIA CREEPER, 60

*W*ALLACE, LILA ACHESON, 14
WALLFLOWERS, 26, 35, 36–37, 41, 43,
    48, 49, 70, 85, 90, 138, *139*
WATER GARDEN, 12, 13, 14, *15*, 19, 21,
    29, 64–65, 104
    BENCHES IN, 53
    BOATS IN, 53, 53–54
    BRIDGES IN, 54–56, *54*, *56*, 67,
        67–68, 70, *71*
    CUP GARDEN CONCEPT OF, 19, 68,
        69, 70
    FOLIAGE EFFECTS IN, 71–72
    JAPANESE INFLUENCE ON, 66–67,
        70, 106
    MONET-STYLE, 76–77
    PAINTINGS OF, 39–40, 55, 56, 76,
        77–78, 79

PATHS IN, 107, 109, *109*
REFLECTIONS IN, 77, 83, 106
SEE ALSO WATER LILIES
WATER LILIES, 12, *16*, 25, 68
    SOURCES OF PLANTS, 17, 35, 74–76, 78
    VARIETIES OF, 74, 75, 77, 78, 138–139
WATER LILIES (MONET), 79
WATER LILY POND, THE (MONET), 54, *55*, 56
WILDFLOWERS, 35
WILLOWS
    POLLARDED, 112–113, *113*
    WEEPING, 64, 68, 72, *102*, 109, 112, 139
WISTERIA, 29, 33, 56, *56*, 57, *57*, 67, 67–68,
    109, 114, 139
WOODRUFF, SWEET, *114*

*Y*ELLOW-VIOLET COLOR HARMONY, 43, *43*

*Z*OLA, EMILE, 21

PHOTOGRAPHY CREDITS

ALL PHOTOGRAPHS: ©DEREK FELL

PAINTINGS AND ILLUSTRATIONS:
ERICH LESSING / ART RESOURCE, NY:
    PP. 55, 79, 84
E.T. ARCHIVE, LONDON: COURTESY OF
    THE MUSEE D'ORSAY PARIS: PP. 31, 39
PHOTOGRAPH ©1983 DETROIT INSTITUTE OF
    THE ARTS, CITY OF DETROIT PURCHASE:
    "GLADIOLI" 1876, CLAUDE MONET: P. 92
©DEREK FELL: P. 97
GIRAUDON / ART RESOURCE, NY: P. 105
PHOTOGRAPH © BOARD OF TRUSTEES,
    NATIONAL GALLERY OF ART, WASHING-
    TON: "THE ARTIST'S GARDEN AT
    VETHEUIL" 1880, CLAUDE MONET: P. 59
NIMATALLAH / ART RESOURCE, NY: P. 108
© STAPELEY WATER GARDENS: P. 17 TOP
UNDERWOOD & UNDERWOOD / CORBIS-
    BETTMANN, NY: P. 8–9
FRONT JACKET: ERICH LESSING / ART
    RESOURCE, NY
BACK JACKET ©PAULA CHAMBREE: TOP
    LEFT, COURTESY OF MUSEE MONET,
    GIVERNY: INSET

GARDEN ILLUSTRATIONS:
JENNIFER MARKSON